# RALPH BACERRA

I AM COMMITTED MORE TO THE IDEA OF PURE BEAUTY.

WHEN IT IS FINISHED, THE PIECE SHOULD BE LIKE AN ORNAMENT, EXQUISITELY BEAUTIFUL.

# RALPH BACERRA
# Exquisite Beauty

**JO LAURIA**

**ESSAYS BY**

Jeannine Falino

Hollis Goodall

Christy Johnson

**OTIS | BEN MALTZ GALLERY**

Otis College of Art and Design

**LOS ANGELES**

Unless otherwise noted, works by Ralph Bacerra are from the collection of Peter and Cindy Bass/Cindy Lee Bass, Executor of the Ralph Bacerra Estate, and are reproduced courtesy of the estate.

This book is published in conjunction with the exhibition *Ralph Bacerra: Exquisite Beauty*, organized by and presented at the Ben Maltz Gallery at Otis College of Art and Design, September 26–December 6, 2015.

The exhibition and publication are funded in part by the National Endowment for the Arts, the Pasadena Art Alliance, and The Boardman Family Foundation. Additional funding has been provided by Friends of Contemporary Ceramics and Japan Art Foundation, Los Angeles.

PUBLISHED BY
Ben Maltz Gallery
Otis College of Art and Design
9045 Lincoln Boulevard
Los Angeles, CA 90045
www.otis.edu/benmaltzgallery
galleryinfo@otis.edu
310.665.6905

ISBN-13: 978-0-930209-41-4

---

PROJECT MANAGER
Jo Lauria

EDITOR
Karen Jacobson

DESIGNER
Amy McFarland, clean{slate}design

PRINTER
Typecraft, Inc., Pasadena, California

This book is printed on #100 text and #130 cover McCoy silk book papers. The text is set in Quadraat, Gotham, and Didot typefaces.

FRONT COVER
*Untitled Platter*, 2007 (detail). Ceramic. Height: 4 in. (10.2 cm); diameter: 28¼ in. (71.8 cm). Collection of David and Julianne Armstrong.

FRONT FLAP
*Untitled Wall Mural*, 1983 (detail). Ceramic. 27½ × 29½ × 3 in. (69.9 × 74.9 × 7.6 cm). Collection of Karen Smits.

BACK COVER
*Cloud Vessel*, 2000 (detail). Porcelain. 22 × 14½ × 6 in. (55.9 × 36.8 × 15.2 cm). Collection of Paul and Sharon Dauer.

BACK FLAP
*Untitled Platter*, 2005 (detail). Ceramic. 3½ × 24½ × 20½ in. (8.9 × 62.2 × 52.1 cm). Collection of Alan Mandell.

PAGE 1
Cup and saucer, from *Untitled Dinnerware*, 1999–2000. Ceramic. Cup: 3¾ × 4¾ × 5¼ in. (9.5 × 12.1 × 13.3 cm); saucer: height: ¾ in. (1.9 cm); diameter: 6¼ in. (15.9 cm).

PAGES 2–3
Untitled, 1998 (detail and full view). Porcelain. 15½ × 19½ × 17⅝ in. (39.4 × 49.5 × 44.8 cm). Collection of Forrest L. Merrill.

---

PAGE 4
Ralph Bacerra in the Chouinard ceramics studio shortly after his appointment as head of ceramics, c. 1968.

PAGE 6
Ralph Bacerra's signature from the underside of the *Dragon Platter* (c. 1975; p. 33).

PAGE 7
Ralph Bacerra applying china paint to a large platter at his Eagle Rock studio, 1974.

PAGE 8
*Untitled Platter*, 2007. Ceramic. Height: 4 in. (10.2 cm); diameter: 28¼ in. (71.8 cm). Collection of David and Julianne Armstrong.

PAGE 9
*Untitled Platter*, 2007. Ceramic. Height: 4 in. (10.2 cm); diameter: 28¼ in. (71.8 cm). Collection of David and Julianne Armstrong.

PAGE 10
*Untitled Platter*, 2007. Ceramic. Height: 4 in. (10.2 cm); diameter: 28¼ in. (71.8 cm).

REPRODUCTION CREDITS
All works by Ralph Bacerra are © the Ralph Bacerra Estate. Other works are © the respective artists. Works by Ralph Bacerra were photographed by David Peters, except as noted below. Photographs in the chronology, other than those of artworks in the exhibition, are from the Ralph Bacerra Archives, except as noted below. Photographs generally appear courtesy of the creators, owners, or lenders of the materials depicted. The following list applies to those for which additional acknowledgments are due.

---

Courtesy American Museum of Ceramic Art: 30, 97

Photo © Asian Art Museum of San Francisco: 31

Courtesy George and Connie Bacerra: 90 (figs. 1–3), 108 (fig. 49)

Courtesy bpk, Berlin / Aegyptisches Museum und Papyrussammlung / Margarete Buesing / Art Resource, NY: 46

© Judy Chicago, 1964. Photo © Donald Woodman: 36 (bottom)

Photo by Jim Cohen; courtesy of Lin Werner: 71, 94 (fig. 20)

Photo by Anthony Cuñha: 10, 50, 61, 62, 68, 69, 86, 96 (fig. 26)

Photo by Ron Cunningham: 108 (fig. 52)

Photo by M. Lee Fatherree: 2, 3, 40, 41, 59, 67

Photo by Richard Gross: 94 (fig. 21), 95 (fig. 23)

Photo by Eva Heyd: 35 (left), 36 (top)

Photo by Marjorie Illig: 105 (fig. 42)

Photo by Wayne Kuwada: 105 (fig. 43)

Photo by Marlea McKinstry: 106 (fig. 45)

Photo © Museum Associates / LACMA: 34 (bottom), 51, 52, 55 (top and bottom), 60, 66 (top)

Photo © Fredrik Nilsen: 34 (top)

Photo by Mac L. Olds: 7

Photo by Sam Parsons: 107 (fig. 47)

Photo by David Peters: 93 (fig. 17)

Courtesy Ralph Bacerra Archives: 4, 7, 14, 22, 66 (bottom), 72

Photo by and courtesy of Porntip Sangvanich: 24 (bottom middle), 112–13

Photo by Gene Sasse: 18

Photo by Gabriel Seri: 1

Unknown photographer: 49, 56, 97 (fig. 28), 101 (fig. 34)

Photo by Ed Watkins: 35 (right)

Photo by John White: 103

# Contents

# Foreword

Ceramic forms, as we see them in the world—whether they are functional, sculptural, or monumental—reflect a fundamental truth about the medium. Simply, clay engages the maker in ways that no other medium can. For fourteen years at Otis College of Art and Design in Los Angeles, Ralph Bacerra (1938–2008) taught young artists and designers additive and subtractive form-making in clay, slip casting, and throwing on the potter's wheel along with glazing and the use of underglazes, overglaze enamels, and metallic lusters. His sumptuously detailed vessels—praised by the critic Ken Johnson for their "visual hedonism"—fed a long tradition of students' and followers' work that, while sometimes appearing fragile, was wholly *permanent* by virtue of its unique material quality. For the combination of fired clay and glaze can result in objects that not only possess great beauty but are weatherproof and tolerant of scorching heat, freezing cold, decades of use and admiration, and sometimes even centuries of burial.

The permanence of ceramic form is an apt metaphor for the extraordinary and vibrant career of Ralph Bacerra. Bacerra—the man, the artist, the teacher, and the program leader—had a long-lasting influence on the development and success of so many students—as did his work itself. His influence reached far beyond his own physical presence among us and continues today to inspire new generations of artists and designers in all mediums.

*Ralph Bacerra: Exquisite Beauty* at Otis's Ben Maltz Gallery is the first major retrospective to showcase and document Bacerra's ceramic vessels and sculptures. It serves as a potent reminder not only of the historical significance of his work but also of the countless hours he dedicated to the design, fabrication, and refined finishing of objects and forms that openly celebrated his true ideal: pure beauty. "When a piece is finished," he told Jo Lauria in a 1994 interview, "it should be like an ornament, exquisitely beautiful."

As an artist and an educator who guides college-level art and design curricula, I can vividly recall my own discovery of Bacerra's work while I was a student of ceramics. Its exemplar status even then—as well as its lush forms, subtle surfaces, and vibrant graphics—motivated me to experiment with fine low-fire finishes in my own work, which later informed my migration from sculpture to painting. I had the pleasure of getting to know Ralph in the early 1980s, when I was a new member of the Otis faculty. Soon I started bringing my first-year three-dimensional design students to his campus studio. He would always thoroughly wow them with demonstrations of the ceramic medium's seemingly magical possibilities.

I am proud that today at Otis, even as we revere the medium of clay in ever-evolving ways, we also remember the significance of Ralph's work and his inspiring influence on so many students and alumni around the world. It is a joy to honor Ralph Bacerra and to reflect on the traditions, as well as the progressive potential, of the medium that he mastered so completely and cherished so deeply.

**RANDALL LAVENDER**
PROVOST, OTIS COLLEGE OF ART AND DESIGN

**Ralph Bacerra**, *Untitled Vessel*, 1999. Porcelain. 20 × 15 × 8 in.
(50.8 × 38.1 × 20.3 cm). Collection of Alan Mandell.

# Introduction

JO LAURIA

*Ralph Bacerra: Exquisite Beauty* is the first retrospective and publication to document the eye-dazzling ceramics created by Ralph Bacerra (1938–2008), a Los Angeles–based artist known for his innovative approach to surface embellishment. The exhibition features more than ninety of the artist's finest pieces—dramatic, highly decorated vessels and sculptures that have never before been the focus of a major exhibition or publication.

Bacerra's career in ceramics spanned five decades, over the course of which his work moved stylistically from traditionalism to pattern and decoration to "post-baroque." He was part of the group of second-generation post–World War II California artists who followed the boundary-expanding lead of Robert Arneson, Viola Frey, John Mason, Ken Price, and Peter Voulkos. These visionary artists sought to use clay in a way that responded to their time and place. Collectively they broadened the possibilities of the medium and brought recognition to the field.

Like those before him, Bacerra regularly challenged ceramic conventions, resolutely experimenting with unfamiliar materials and techniques in his studio. His unique contribution was the creation of a new "grammar of ornament" through the complex layering of aggregated design motifs, achieved primarily through multiple applications of underglazes and overglazes combined with metallic lusters. The resultant interweave generated a language rich in cross-cultural inflection and design schemes fluent in optically inventive patterns that played with perception and teased the eye.

Ralph Bacerra was born on January 23, 1938, in Garden Grove, California; his father was from the Philippines, his mother from Montana. He attended what is now Orange Coast College in Costa Mesa, California, and in 1957 enrolled at Chouinard Art Institute in Los Angeles, where he initially studied graphic design. An elective class in ceramics, however, altered Bacerra's life: after one semester of study with Vivika Heino, a pioneering studio potter and celebrated educator, he veered away from commercial art.

Ralph Bacerra on the front porch of his home in Eagle Rock, c. 1963.

Bacerra had taken a studio class in pottery at Orange Coast College but hadn't realized or considered that ceramics could be a vocation. Heino and her husband, Otto, worked together at the Chouinard ceramics studio, although only Vivika was formally engaged as an instructor. They collaborated on the making, glazing, and firing of their pieces, extending this practice to their home studio, where they also displayed and sold their pottery (left). This opened Bacerra's eyes to the possibilities of a profession in ceramics, and the Heinos became his lifelong mentors. In an interview the artist recalled his early experience with Vivika Heino in the Chouinard ceramics studio: "And once she started to talk, demonstrate, and the environment in the classroom, and I started to get more serious of working with the wheel and the clay and the glazes. I said this is for me. This is where I want to be, and I dropped everything and switched my major to ceramics."[1]

When Vivika Heino accepted a teaching position at Rhode Island School of Design in 1963, she recommended Bacerra as her replacement. He served as the head of ceramics at Chouinard from 1964 through 1971, when the school was formally absorbed into California Institute of the Arts and the ceramics major was eliminated from the curriculum.

**Ralph Bacerra**, drawing from sketchbook, 1957–58. Graphite, ink, and pen on paper. 11 × 8 in. (27.9 × 20.3 cm).

Vivika Heino, head of the ceramics department, working in the studio, Chouinard Art Institute, 1959.

Otto Heino throwing a large platter on the potter's wheel in the Chouinard ceramics studio, 1959.

Chouinard was a proving ground for Bacerra both as a student and as a teacher. As he matured in the classroom—he was only twenty-six years old when he became department head—his ceramics also became more sophisticated and refined. His elegant Asian-inspired porcelain vases and bottles caught the attention of Ken Deavers, founder of the American Hand gallery in Washington, DC. In 1967 Deavers invited Bacerra to join the gallery's roster of artists. This relationship, which continued until 1997, provided Bacerra with representation on the East Coast and increased visibility as a ceramist.

Bacerra's recognition was furthered in the late 1960s and early 1970s, when his work became identified with the art movement "variously known as 'Finish Fetish' or 'Fetish Finish' depending on whether the emphasis was on the obsessive preciousness of the art object or on its pristine surface."[2] In ceramics, this style demanded that the work be flawlessly executed and deliberately seductive in both shape and surface. *Orange Form* (1968; left), with its sensuous contours and enticing glaze treatment, is emblematic of this aesthetic direction. Although Bacerra felt that too much was made of his association with this style, it is clear that he believed in its underlying principles: "Technique is a high priority. The skill has to be evident in each piece. That is to say that the form should be pleasing, the glaze and the colors are right and the design is completely worked-out."[3]

After his teaching job at Chouinard was eliminated, Bacerra spent the next decade as a full-time studio artist. This was a time of intense experimentation. Dating from this period are the handsome covered stoneware jars (p. 18) and the intriguing mythical animal sculptures

**Ralph Bacerra**, *Orange Form*, 1968. Earthenware, metallic (chrome, lead) overglaze; wheel-thrown. 9½ × 9 × 8¾ in. (24.1 × 22.9 × 22.2 cm). Museum of Arts and Design, New York; Gift of the Johnson Wax Company, through the American Craft Council, 1977 (1977.2.6).

This sensuous sculpture was selected by curator Lee Nordness for *Objects: USA*. The exhibition opened at the Smithsonian Institution in 1969 before beginning an extensive US tour, eventually crossing the Atlantic and traveling to European venues.

that illustrate his curiosity and whimsicality (see pp. 66–67). The animal sculptures mark an important development in his work. They were perhaps the first series in which he blended his exceptional craftsmanship with the ability to express narrative: each sculpture evokes a sense of place, story, and attitude.

Bacerra also took advantage of his more open schedule to travel to Asia, visiting Japan, Taiwan, Korea, Hong Kong, Singapore, and the Philippines. On return trips to Japan he had the opportunity to closely examine historical Japanese ceramics, specifically Imari, Kutani, and Nabeshima wares. In Taiwan, he sought out ceramics from China's Song, Tang, and Ming dynasties in the collection of the National Palace Museum, Taipei, with a special focus on the extensive selection of celadon-glazed vessels and on the shapes and glaze variations in the blue-and-white porcelains of the fourteenth through seventeenth centuries. His gaze

Above: **Ralph Bacerra**, *Green Casserole*, c. 1973. Stoneware. Lid: height: 3 in. (7.6 cm); diameter: 11 in. (27.9 cm). Base: height: 5¾ in. (14.6 cm); diameter: 11 in. (27.9 cm). Long Beach Museum of Art, Long Beach, CA, Gift of Garth Clark and Mark Del Vecchio.

Above, right: **Ralph Bacerra**, *Covered Vessel with Handles*, 1975. Porcelain. Height: 15 in. (38.1 cm); diameter: 9½ in. (24.1 cm). Collection of Ken Deavers.

was also aroused by the rich colors, abstract designs, and repeating patterns of Japanese textiles and the boldly graphic woodblock prints of nineteenth-century Japanese ukiyo-e masters such as Katsushika Hokusai. This exploration of historical Asian ceramics, textiles, and prints informed his work, and he began to create original pieces that drew inspiration from them (above). Other sources that influenced Bacerra's design vocabulary were the pottery traditions of Ottoman Turkey, especially Iznik ceramics; Persian miniatures; the drawings of the Dutch graphic artist M. C. Escher; and the geometric patterns that pervaded early modernism. Bacerra's particular delight in the sensuously decorative late "gold paintings" of the Austrian artist Gustav Klimt is reflected in his densely patterned ceramics (p. 20).

The second phase of Bacerra's teaching career began in 1982 at the invitation of Otis Art Institute. The first year he taught part-time, leading classes in surface design and glaze technology. The following year he was appointed chair of ceramics with oversight of all aspects of the ceramics studio. He held the position for thirteen years, teaching a new generation of students the skills necessary to become successful studio artists and educators. All who spent time in his classroom benefited from his technical expertise and keen design sensibility. Many of his former students from both Chouinard and Otis have ascended to prominence in the ceramics field and have contributed to its vitality. Bacerra retired from teaching in 1996, when Otis relocated and discontinued ceramics as a core discipline.

Above: **Ralph Bacerra**, *Untitled Platter*, 1982. Porcelain. Height: 3 in. (7.6 cm); diameter: 19 in. (48.3 cm). Collection of Ted Rowland.

The finely delineated design of the blue-and-white drawing on this platter clearly demonstrates Bacerra's skill at executing this traditional Chinese technique of underglaze blue-and-white painting, which is achieved through the application of cobalt oxide.

While he was still at Otis, Bacerra's work took a new direction with a series of platters and sculptural bowls. Essentially the artist permitted the volumetric dimensions of the piece and its profile to dictate the design treatment. "Surface follows form" was one of his teaching mantras and a guiding principle of his work. The rims of platters were cut in geometric shapes, and double-walled vessels and chargers were embellished with protrusions that were aligned with the geometry of the surface design (below). These extensions created a constant interplay between three-dimensional volume and two-dimensional surface design. The overall effect is one of visual stimulation and excitement. As Bacerra himself commented: "There is playfulness in this work. Shapes jump out and recede. They move forward and go back. They intertwine with

Opposite, left: **Ralph Bacerra**, *Untitled Teapot*, 1998. Earthenware. 17 × 13 × 10 in. (43.2 × 33 × 25.4 cm). Collection of Ken Deavers.

The multiple patterns covering this teapot pay homage to several design sources, which Bacerra adeptly combined and refined to arrive at an exuberant personal style of decoration.

Above: **Ralph Bacerra**, *Untitled Portrait Charger*, 1993. Ceramic. 7⅝ × 25¾ × 25 in. (19.4 × 65.4 × 63.5 cm). Collection of Anne Cohen Ruderman and David Ruderman.

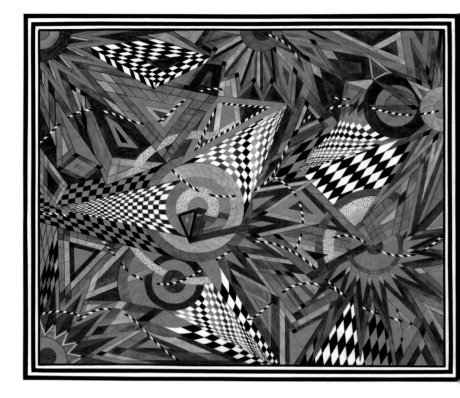

one another. Seemingly flat surfaces become dimensional. Straight lines become curved. Most people don't understand this unless they become involved in the work."[4]

Liberated from full-time teaching in 1996, Bacerra was able to return to his studio and concentrate wholly on his art practice. From the mid-1990s through the early 2000s, he focused on creating new series of artworks for annual exhibitions at Garth Clark Gallery in New York and Frank Lloyd Gallery in Santa Monica, California. Collectors and curators responded enthusiastically to his solo exhibitions, and as a result, work was placed in important private and public collections in the United States and abroad, enhancing his international reputation. Additionally, critics frequently reviewed these shows, and their assessments validated his work and helped to affirm his standing in the art community. During this period of intense focus, Bacerra also executed several private and public art commissions. *Kaloseidos (Beauty and Form)*—a ceramic mural commissioned by Maguire Partners for Western Asset Plaza in Pasadena, California—is a tour de force of design and engineering: more than three thousand individual tiles create an intricate pattern of colorful, animated geometric forms that optically project and retreat in a lively interchange with viewer perception (p. 111).

———————

Bacerra's virtuosic works demonstrated a mastery of materials, consummate craftsmanship, and an innate understanding of the holistic unity of form and surface decoration. He became the undisputed master of the ornamental in ceramics, distinguishing himself, in the words of the historian of ceramics Garth Clark, as the "most extraordinary decorative potter of the last fifty years."[5] Regrettably, a major survey or retrospective at a public institution eluded Bacerra during his lifetime, and until now there was no monograph devoted to his prodigious output.

In addition to presenting work from throughout Bacerra's career, this volume examines his accomplishments from varied perspectives. Jeannine Falino frames his innovative use of overglaze enamels within the context of the history of American china painting and the pattern and decoration movement of the 1970s. Hollis Goodall assesses the cross-cultural influences in the artist's work, focusing on his engagement with the ceramic traditions of Asia, especially his adaptation of the patterns and palette of Japanese ceramics. Christy Johnson examines his influence as a teacher and highlights the accomplishments of his students. In the illustrated chronology, Bacerra's life is chronicled through photographs of the artist and his family and associates, images of significant works, and documentation of his professional

**Ralph Bacerra**, Rendering for *Kaloseidos (Beauty and Form)*, 2003. Watercolor on paper. 40 × 28 in. (101.6 × 71.1 cm) framed.

Bacerra created this original rendering as part of a proposal for a commissioned ceramic mural for Western Asset Plaza, Pasadena, California. He received the commission and executed the tile mural (p. 111). The finished mural, spanning twelve by sixteen feet, is installed on the east-facing wall of the plaza.

achievements, offering the reader an intimate view of an extraordinary career, decade by decade. "Remembering Ralph Bacerra" presents recollections and reflections by Bacerra's friends and colleagues.

Bacerra had an artistic direction and vision that were constant. His aesthetic compass was always pointed toward beauty as he saw it: manifested in nature; expressed through organic, abstract, and geometric forms; and mediated through the harmony of composition, pattern, and color. When the notion of beauty came under fire and was out of fashion in art, he clung to his inspiration, and his work remained unabashedly decorative. His lifelong pursuit was the creation of eloquent, highly refined objects with resplendent surfaces, which he hoped would bring pleasure to all who engaged with them. In this pursuit the artist was sublimely successful: to gaze intently on a Bacerra artwork is to be rewarded with an exquisite visual experience.

**NOTES**

**1.** Ralph Bacerra, oral history interview conducted by Frank Lloyd, April 7–19, 2004, Archives of American Art, Smithsonian Institution.
**2.** Frances Colpitt, "The Optimistic Object: L.A. Art in the 1960s," in *Finish Fetish: LA's Cool School* (Los Angeles: Fisher Gallery, University of Southern California, 1991), 6.
**3.** Ralph Bacerra, in Jo Lauria, "Ralph Bacerra—Ceramic Artist," *Ceramics: Art and Perception*, no. 15 (1994): 15.
**4.** Ibid., 18.
**5.** Garth Clark, "Ralph Bacerra, 1938–2008," *Ceramics Monthly* 56 (February 2008): 48.

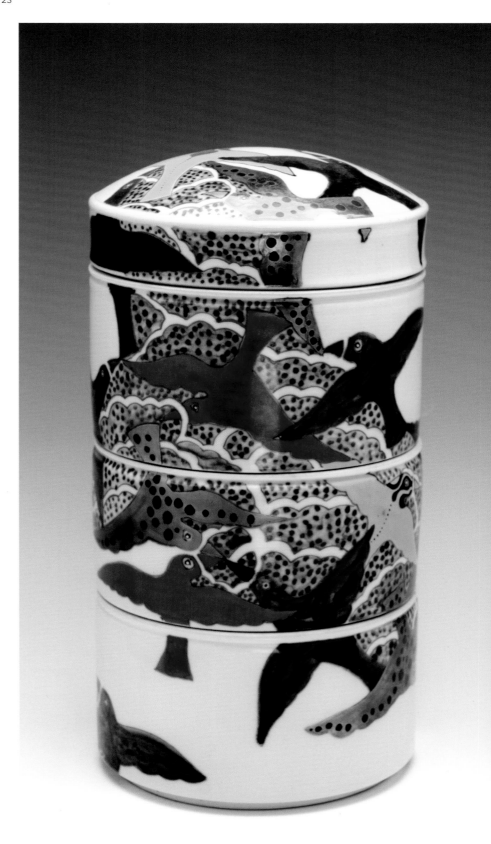

**Ralph Bacerra**, *Untitled Stacking Covered Vessel*, 1977. Porcelain. Height: 13 in. (33 cm); diameter: 6½ in. (16.5 cm). Collection of Susan Steinhauser and Dan Greenberg.

The repeating pattern of birds in flight against dotted clouds rendered in bold yellow, red, blue, and gold metallic luster shows the influence of historical Japanese Imari designs and the characteristic palette of overglaze enamels.

# The Eagle Rock and the Mound Series | 1968

JO LAURIA

The first home and studio that Ralph Bacerra owned were located in the Eagle Rock neighborhood of Los Angeles, directly below, and in the shadow of, the famous rock after which the area was named (below left). Bacerra was a great admirer of the wild landscape that surrounded his property and was an adventurous gardener, cultivating many species of flora, especially cacti and succulents, several of which were exotic. He delighted in making handcrafted pots in which to grow and showcase his plants, and these pots enlivened his landscape (below center).

Early in his studio career, Bacerra would position his vessels on a table on an outdoor porch and photograph them against the backdrop of the majestic Eagle Rock (below right). This massive boulder also served as the inspiration for his first series of organic sculptures, begun in 1968. The mound shapes that make up this series—variously titled *Orange Form, Orange Form 2*, and so on—represented a pivotal moment: Bacerra closed the openings of the vessels, deliberately denying their function. The mound-like vessels were hand-built as hollow forms, shaped to echo the surrounding mountains, hills, and rock formations. These mounds were not finished in earth tones or a naturalistic palette, however, but were decorated with brilliant colored glazes—some smooth, some textured—and further surfaced with patterns created using overglaze enamels and metallic lusters. Through this process Bacerra created a strong visual dynamic between the amorphous shape and the organic abstract designs that flowed over the shoulder and swirled to the top of the mound, leading the eye to the pinnacle, where the excitement culminated.

Top: **Ralph Bacerra**, *Orange Form 2*, 1968. Earthenware, glaze, overglaze enamels. 10 × 9 × 8 in. (25.4 × 22.9 × 20.3 cm). Private collection.

Above, left: A photograph that Bacerra took from his backyard looking up at the Eagle Rock.

Above, middle: Handcrafted ceramic garden pot in Bacerra's backyard, 2008.

Above, right: Bacerra's glazed stoneware teapot (1970), photographed in his backyard with the Eagle Rock in the distance.

**Ralph Bacerra**, *Orange Form 3*, 1968. Earthenware, glaze,
overglaze enamels. 10 × 8½ × 8¾ in. (25.4 × 21.6 × 22.2 cm).
Private collection.

**Ralph Bacerra**, *Teapot*, n.d. Earthenware. 20 × 12 × 17 in. (50.8 × 30.5 × 43.2 cm). Collection of Sonny and Gloria Kamm.

**Ralph Bacerra**, *Cloud Teapot*, 1998. Whiteware. 21 × 20 × 5 in. (53.3 × 50.8 × 12.7 cm). Collection of Alan Mandell.

# The Low Made High

## RALPH BACERRA, PATTERN DECORATION, AND CHINA PAINTING

JEANNINE FALINO

The brilliantly patterned ceramics of Ralph Bacerra are a high point in the modern history of china painting. His artistic journey was rooted in the study of Asian pottery and textiles, Persian manuscripts, and modern abstraction, cultivated through travel, collecting, and close examination and fueled by a deep knowledge of glaze chemistry. In the process, Bacerra developed a distinctively dense and abstract approach to the pattern decoration of ceramics and set a modern standard for the field.

To better understand Bacerra's contributions, it is useful to consider his accomplishments against the backdrop of American china painting before his time. It was a bold move for a modern ceramist to choose china painting, also known as overglaze painting, a process that involves firing mineral-based colors to a previously glazed clay body, because of its long association in the West with the low, applied, or minor arts.[1] Moreover, china painting had a complex cultural history in the United States. In the nineteenth century it was linked to women's domestic activities like quilting and lace making.[2] Despite the fact that the first teachers of the technique were men, born and trained abroad, it was not appreciated as an art form in this country because of

its perceived amateur status. In the twentieth century, china painting was largely the purview of hobby groups and considered beneath the consideration of the art world until it was taken up by a tiny minority working in higher education during the 1960s and 1970s.

Just as unusual was Bacerra's decision to emphasize the decorated surface. Abstraction had dominated the art world for decades. It was not until the 1960s—when a convergence of activity associated with "finish fetish," funk, feminism, and the pattern and decoration movement challenged the minimalist paradigm—that it became possible for a new generation of artists to embrace ornament.[3] As these movements gained momentum, Bacerra made similar advances in the realm of ceramics. Yet even in this familiar environment, he charted an independent route. Not only was decoration shunned by the broader art world, it was also avoided by most midcentury ceramists who embraced the concept of the "humble pot," epitomized by the deliberately minimal and organically shaped vessels of Karen Karnes, Robert Turner, and Marguerite Wildenhain. The humble pot was paralleled by the Japanese *mingei*, or folk art, movement, which had an extended influence on

Ralph Bacerra, *Vessel/Violet*, 1988. Glazed earthenware with lusters. 11½ × 22 × 22 in. (29.2 × 55.9 × 55.9 cm). Arizona State University Art Museum; Museum purchase through a gift from the Stéphane Janssen Art Foundation.

American potters when the influential Japanese potter Shōji Hamada made tours of the United States in 1952 and 1963. Bacerra attended Hamada's 1963 presentation at the University of Southern California and recorded the event with a sketch of the artist at work (above left). Hamada's glistening but muted brown iron-saturated and *tenmoku* glazes were widely respected, as were his calligraphic lines that acted as elegant foils to these sober backgrounds. Bacerra followed this aesthetic early in his career, using his brush to evoke the movement of birds in the sky or fluttering leaves in the wind (above right).

A broader interest in color and pattern-based ornament had just begun to emerge when Bacerra graduated from Chouinard Art Institute in 1961. As a student of Vivika Heino, he was rigorously trained in glaze chemistry, especially in the nuances of matching glazes to clay bodies and temperatures.[4] He benefited from meetings held by the American Ceramic Society with many of the leading ceramists of Southern California in attendance, including Laura Andreson, Susan Peterson, and Peter Voulkos.[5]

Vivika and Otto Heino took Bacerra under their wing, bringing him along on at least one road trip to their summer home in New Hampshire. As they stopped at museums along the way, Bacerra saw a quantity of international ceramics and gravitated toward Asian works finished in a variety of decorative patterns. A telling story comes from the gallerist Frank Lloyd, who recalled a vessel shown to him by Vivika Heino that appeared to be Chinese but was in fact an early example by Bacerra. This sort of close observation was to serve Bacerra well when he made visits to the Asian Art Museum of San Francisco. He would study the museum's Treasure Wall, which held a wide selection of Chinese ceramics from the permanent collection, offering a rich panoply of

**Ralph Bacerra**, *Sketch of Shoji Hamada at a Hamada Workshop at the University of Southern California, Sept. 1963*, 1963. Ink on paper. 10⅝ × 8¼ in. (27 × 21 cm). Ralph Bacerra papers, 1959–2003, Archives of American Art, Smithsonian Institution.

**Ralph Bacerra**, *Round-Bodied Covered Jar*, c. 1970. Stoneware. Height: 17½ in. (44. 5 cm); diameter: 11 in. (27.9 cm). The American Museum of Ceramic Art, Gift of James W. and Jackie Voell, 2005.2.0033.

materials, techniques, colors, and patterns for contemplation (above).[6]

In the 1950s and 1960s stoneware was the prevailing clay body used by American ceramics departments, including the one at Chouinard. A high-fire material, stoneware was combined with generally brown, gray, or cream-colored glazes that could withstand such heat. At the beginning of his career, Bacerra worked in stoneware too, throwing sturdy vessels, some adorned with calligraphic brushwork in Hamada's style.[7] By the 1970s Bacerra had begun to experiment with pattern-based decoration. Since he had studied commercial art prior to taking up ceramics and had considered a career as a graphic designer, the integration of a flat pattern with three-dimensional clay forms must have strongly appealed to him (p. 32). One of his early successes was a lidded stoneware jar featuring a cobalt dragon-like creature in a bold sgraffito design (p. 33, top). This motif appeared elsewhere in various combinations

and different techniques—as in the dynamic *Dragon Platter* in porcelain, executed several years later (p. 33, bottom)—all with obvious references to the Asian sources that he had come to love.

Having mastered these early compositions using one or two colors, Bacerra began to apply his talents in glaze chemistry to enlarge his palette and widen his design vocabulary. Understanding the principles of overglaze decoration and having examined a number of Asian examples, he also knew that it was necessary to shift from stoneware to a porous-bodied whiteware or porcelain, on which the glazes would achieve greater brilliance.[8]

A major turning point came in 1980, when Bacerra took his first trip to Asia.[9] Over the course of his travels to Japan, South Korea, Hong Kong, and Taiwan, he had the opportunity to examine quantities of ceramics with overglaze decoration. He particularly enjoyed seeing

Installation view of the Treasure Wall at the Asian Art Museum, Golden Gate Park, San Francisco.

**Ralph Bacerra**, *Study of Birds*, c. 1980. Gouache on paper. 18 × 24 in. (45.7 × 61 cm).

**Ralph Bacerra**, *Untitled Covered Jar*, 1969. Glazed stoneware. Height: 18 in. (45.7 cm); diameter: 13 in. (33 cm).

**Ralph Bacerra**, *Dragon Platter*, c. 1975. Porcelain. 1 × 14 × 7½ in. (2.5 × 35.6 × 19.1 cm). Collection of Lin Werner.

the ceramics at the National Palace Museum in Taipei, the repository of many of China's greatest cultural treasures. While in Nagoya, Japan, he purchased his first set of overglaze enamels and brushes, marking the beginning of his odyssey in surface decoration using these materials.

As Bacerra was making his own transition to overglaze painting, he joined a small but influential group of ceramic artists working with intense colors. Most of them hailed from the West Coast, where there was a greater willingness to reject East Coast–based minimalism. In Los Angeles, Kenneth Price had been a painting and ceramics student who had briefly studied with Peter Voulkos. As early as 1959 he began to react against Voulkos's heroic scale and dark glazes by making considerably smaller, curiously primordial objects out of clay with surfaces covered in saturated, acid colors made with low-fire commercial glazes or acrylic paint, often focusing on the "linear edge" and the creation of negative space around the object (top right).[10] Price was associated with the famously subversive group represented by the Ferus Gallery, which included Larry Bell, Billy Al Bengston, Robert Irwin, and Craig Kaufmann, who adopted plastic, resin, glass, fiberglass, and automotive paint, glossy materials typically associated with cars and surfboards, which led their work to be labeled "finish fetish."

In the Bay Area, Ron Nagle had been inspired by Price and, like him, experimented endlessly with tiny cups saturated with rich colors and decals (bottom right). Nagle's mother regularly hosted a china-painting club in the family's basement, and he soon mastered the technique for his own purposes. Nagle was aware of how dated and even dowdy china painting appeared:

Kenneth Price (United States, 1935–2012), *Snail Cup*, 1968. Glazed ceramic. 2⅞ × 5¼ × 2⅝ in. (7.3 × 13.3 × 6.7 cm). Los Angeles County Museum of Art, Art Museum Council Fund, M.83.230.60.

Ron Nagle (United States b. 1939), *Untitled (Turkey-Toss Box Cup)*, 1996. Porcelain, mixed media. Cup: height: 3 in. (7.6 cm); diameter: 5 in. (12.7 cm). Box: 13 × 13 × 4 in. (33 × 33 × 10.7 cm). Los Angeles County Museum of Art, Smits Ceramics Purchase Fund AC1997.57.1.1–.2.

I still use the techniques today, but things that are peculiar to the hobbyist, like slip-casting and china painting and low-fire ceramics and bright colors and all this stuff. I mean, these are things—and decals. All of that stuff was stuff that [my mother] was doing in the early '50s with a bunch of women in the basement, and at the time of abstract expressionism and then the new clay movement, which was starting. It was—that would have been considered very uncool, you know, to use any of that stuff. So, I mean, I was interested, and—but not that much, you know? I just sort of gravitated towards it. [11]

It was Nagle, then teaching at the San Francisco Art Institute with Jim Melchert, who changed the focus of the ceramics department from stoneware to low-fire clay. One of Nagle's most successful students in this regard was Richard Shaw, whose investigation of the medium led to a National Endowment for the Arts grant to develop ceramic inks for use at low temperatures. This technical knowledge allowed him to combine elements of printed matter in dazzling trompe l'oeil fashion, a format that he has explored ever since (above left). Similarly, the new funk ceramics pioneered in the early 1960s by Robert Arneson inverted the stoneware standard by using low-fire whiteware, along with commercial glazes typically associated with hobby shops, to explore new work (above right). In Seattle, at the University of Washington, Howard Kottler contrasted flaming hot colors with luster glazes in the 1960s (p. 36, top), and his student Patty Warashina followed suit with a series of surrealistic meditations on American life. Color was employed by these artists to enhance form, create narrative, or for imitative purposes; none considered using decorative pattern to create surface interest.[12]

Richard Shaw (United States, b. 1941), *Couch and Chair with Landscape and Cows*, 1966–67. Earthenware, acrylic paint, wood, leather. Chair: 9 × 10 × 5 3/4 in. (22.9 × 25.4 × 14.6 cm). Sofa: 9¾ × 18½ × 10 in. (24.8 × 47 × 25.4 cm). Museum of Arts and Design, Gift of the Johnson Wax Company, through the American Craft Council, 1977.

Robert Arneson (United States, 1930–1992), *Box House Landscape with a View of Alice and "L,"* 1966. Polychrome earthenware, hand-built, glazed, underglaze painted. 15½ × 11 × 9¼ in. (39.4 × 27.9 × 23.5 cm). Museum of Arts and Design, Gift of the artist, through the American Craft Council, 1968.

free to explore decoration until long after the 1960s. There seemed to be little place in this modern world of "arctic purity" for the delicacy and richness of overglaze decoration, with its vibrant colors and varied patterns and designs.[14]

Fortunately abstraction was losing ground. By the 1970s many in the art world were rejecting canonical ideas about avant-garde art and exploring the richness of color, design, and pattern, including that found in china painting. While not formally associated with the Ferus group, Judy Chicago, then working in Los Angeles, was one of many in the region who discovered the joys of acrylic lacquer paints when she produced *Car Hood* in 1964, painting brightly colored patterns on an actual Corvair hood (below). Chicago's search for saturated color brought her into contact with china painters, who were mostly women

The independent paths chosen by these artists presented a powerfully attractive and subversive response to abstraction, which had held sway in the art world for decades. Beginning with "Avant-garde and Kitsch" (1939), the New York critic Clement Greenberg had codified a binary relationship between "low" art forms such as decorative painting, which he considered kitsch, in contrast to abstract expressionism and other modernist forms, which he regarded as "high" art.[13] Greenberg's writings cast a long shadow that encouraged orthodoxy across mediums and hindered pluralistic modes of expression. This had an influence on artists working in craft, many of whom did not feel

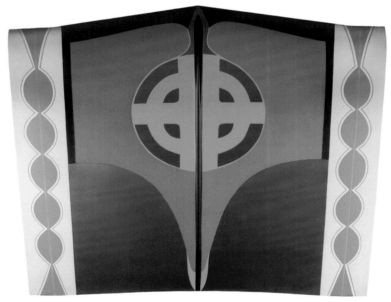

Howard Kottler (United States, 1930–1989), *Empress Jar*, 1967. Stoneware, low-fire glazes, luster glaze. 12¾ × 15 × 7½ in. (32.4 × 38.1 × 19.1 cm). Museum of Arts and Design, Gift of the artist, through the American Craft Council, 1967.

Judy Chicago (United States, b. 1939), *Car Hood*, 1964. Sprayed acrylic lacquer on Corvair car hood. 42¹⁵⁄₁₆ × 49³⁄₁₆ × 4⁵⁄₁₆ in. (109.2 × 125 × 111.3 cm). Moderna Museet, Stockholm. Acquired 2007 with means from The Second Museum of Our Wishes.

artists working in a "nonauthoritarian" cooperative atmosphere, much like nineteenth-century practitioners. The gendered nature of the medium fit her vision for her iconic work titled *The Dinner Party*, created in Los Angeles between 1974 and 1979, which was dominated by china-painted dinner plates.[15] Bacerra may have seen the installation during its 1979 premiere at the San Francisco Museum of Modern Art.

Chicago was friendly with members of the pattern and decoration movement, which held its first meeting in 1976 in Los Angeles, where a communal desire was expressed for "humanistic and decorative themes that had been excluded from the domain of modernism."[16] Its members were men and women painters who rebelled against minimalism and wanted to inject their work with content drawn from the world around them and their personal lives. Some were feminists, like Joyce Kozloff, who was glad to learn that her interest in pattern was not confined to women. She infused her work (right) with design motifs from non-Western cultures gleaned from her travels, finding it "more lively and interesting (aesthetically) to be inclusive than exclusive."[17] Like fellow pattern and decoration artist Miriam Shapiro, who shifted from painting to textile-based compositions, Kozloff moved away from painting to experiment with printmaking and ceramic tiles, and her work in the 1979 Whitney Biennial included columns of brilliant tiles. By the 1980s she had begun a series of public installations made of decorative tile. The first of them, at the international terminal at San Francisco International Airport (1983), celebrated the city's Victorian residences, deco architecture, and funk culture in its decorative scheme.[18]

Top: **Joyce Kozloff** (United States, b. 1942), *Medersa El-Attarin, Fez, with Secession Trees and Water*, 1985. Watercolor on paper. 30 × 22 in. (76.2 × 55.8 cm). Courtesy of the artist and DC Moore Gallery, New York.

Bottom: **Joyce Kozloff** (United States, b. 1942), *An Interior Decorated*, 1978–79 (detail). Hand-painted glazed ceramic tiles grouted on wood. 126 × 174 × 4½ in. (320 × 442 × 11.4 cm). Ludwig Forum für Internationale Kunst, Aachen, Germany. Installation view, Mint Museum, Charlotte, North Carolina, 1980.

While the pattern and decoration movement has been categorized as short-lived and confined to a limited number of participants, its influence has in fact been widespread and continues to multiply.[19] For the first time since the Aesthetic Era in the late nineteenth century, a method of expression was put forth that valued rhythm, color, pattern, and culture, and this proved irresistible in an increasingly global society.

Bacerra was an artistic beneficiary of these consciousness-raising efforts. Los Angeles was a hub of visual arts ferment in those years, and these developments could not have escaped him. A participant in the city's visual arts scene and yet set apart by his singular love for Asian ceramics, he had moved decisively from simple, blue-and-white or green-and-white designs to a well-controlled explosion of color. Claiming that he had no need for preparatory work such as detailed drawings for his compositions, Bacerra nevertheless employed stencils to draw patterns of irises, rabbits, fish, and birds, among other stylized flora and fauna, on his bisque ware.[20] He managed an elaborate firing schedule to accommodate the temperature requirements for each color. Some glazes were refired to obtain the desired saturation, while others were fired at successively cooler temperatures, ending with the lowest temperatures for luster glazes. Sometimes as many as fourteen firings were required for a single object, and the labor-intensive process was fraught with the potential for breakage and flaws in the kiln.

During his first teaching stint at the Chouinard Art Institute, where he took over from Vivika Heino in 1963, Bacerra mentored a very receptive and imaginative group of students—including Juanita Jimenez, Jun Kaneko, Mineo Mizuno, Don Pilcher, Elsa Rady, Adrian Saxe, and Peter Shire—impressing them with the power of colored glazes and the importance of matching surface to volume through a deep understanding of glaze chemistry. At Chouinard and later, while working independently in his studio, Bacerra continued his explorations of surface design. In terms of compositions, he adopted a layered effect in which dense patterns appeared to overlap one another in a spreading fashion. At the same time he expanded his vocabulary of forms to images of clouds, birds, and pinwheels with hatchwork and stipplework to provide background patterns. He adapted an M. C. Escher–like technique to depict pattern migrations with great success. New breakthroughs came when he included several large and differing fields of patterns or designs within a single composition, covering the entire surface of the object, as with his Iris platter of 1978, using Imari-inspired colors (opposite).[21] With time, the vessels and patterns grew larger and more complex, as did the relationship of the vessel form to pattern, the power of deep space, and, following his interest in Escher, intensive experimentation with designs that pushed and pulled the eye in unexpected ways.

From the time of his appointment in 1982 to the ceramics faculty at Otis Art Institute of Parsons School of Design (now Otis College of Art and Design) until his retirement in 1996, Bacerra actively promoted and taught an East Asian aesthetic, with an emphasis on glaze application. His students included Keiko Fukazawa, Michael Johns, Cindy Kolodziejski, Diego Romero, Scott and Naomi Schoenherr, Porntip Sangvanich, and Joan Takayama-Ogawa, some of whom have followed his intensive interest in surface decoration to new ends.[22] A demanding teacher, he used his own collection of ceramics as a teaching tool,

**Ralph Bacerra**, *Iris Platter*, c. 1978. White stoneware.
16 × 10 × 10 in. (40.6 × 25.4 × 25.4 cm). Collection of
Lin Werner.

challenging his students to critically evaluate and re-create historical glazes. Bacerra was so highly regarded that the ceramist and historian Susan Peterson requested a series of plates demonstrating his china-painting technique as illustrations for her landmark book *The Craft and Art of Clay* (1992); the four plates, which are somewhat analogous to "states" in printmaking, show his painstaking process (above).[23]

Throughout his career Bacerra remained steadfastly faithful to the concept of beauty, with a resolute disinterest in commentary or narrative, unlike many of his peers, and with only the briefest of forays into figurative art, such as his richly colored walking figures from the 1970s (p. 86) and his portrait heads of the 1990s (p. 42). His search for beauty was rooted in widely divergent places, such as Imari porcelain

and the brilliant geometric compositions of the artists known as the Blue Four—Lionel Feininger, Alexei Jawlensky, Vasily Kandinsky, and Paul Klee—whose works were on view at the Pasadena Art Museum.[24] Bacerra often visited the museum, and a Kandinsky poster was permanently installed in his studio.[25] It is perhaps no surprise that the paintings of Gustav Klimt also appealed to him, for the two shared a keen interest in dense pattern enlivened with gold that Bacerra investigated with overglaze colors and luster. The artist recalled:

**Ralph Bacerra**, *Set of Four Demonstration China-Painting Plates*, c. 1990. Ceramic. Height: 1 in. (2.5 cm); diameter: 12 in. (30.5 cm) each. Collection of Forrest L. Merrill.

[The Blue Four were] always on display at the Pasadena Art Museum, where I used to visit quite often, and that's a big influence in my painting and in my design. Also, M. C. Escher from Holland for his interlocking shapes that form shapes within shapes that all sort of interlock like a puzzle. Persian paintings as well, Persian manuscripts. Japanese prints—you can pick up patterns and different kinds of ways that they have a blank space and then a pattern and gold. And these are all sort of influences that I don't really think about, but once I've done them and I see the piece, I say, well, you know, there's certain Japanese or a Persian influence here, Escher here, Kandinsky there maybe. But all those things are sort of intuitive, I think. You do research, you read books, you see the shows, and they're sort of in the back of your head, and as you begin to work, it all begins to come out. [26]

By the late 1980s Bacerra had synthesized these influences into a design language featuring circles, triangles, stripes, and checkerboards that appeared to be zooming into and out of the viewer's space. These new designs became the basis for his mature work and appeared on cubist-inspired chargers and vessels with exaggerated edges or bulging sides that fairly danced in place. The results were a vertigo-inducing, dizzying, wild, visual roller-coaster ride that left the viewer gasping for air—and wanting more. Sometimes using celadon glazes on cloud-shaped or cubist forms, Bacerra created a cool oasis that contrasted with pattern. Other celadon glazes adorned pierced porcelain forms that conjured an Asian sensibility of his own creation. As he moved in series from teapots to plates to covered jars and his magnificent

portrait heads, he created hallucinogenic storms of mind-bending complexity, always striving for an opulently and openly beautiful decorated surface that held no hidden meanings or social agenda beyond sheer artistry.

Ralph Bacerra's dazzling fusion of surface designs with impeccable craftsmanship makes him a compelling artist for any age. By combining far-flung design sources into a unique visual vocabulary and executing them in overglaze enamels, he transformed a formerly "low" or minor technique into "high" art. With his wholehearted and unabashed embrace of pattern and color, Bacerra helped to unlock a long-barred door to a secret garden of profound grace and beauty.

**Ralph Bacerra**, *Portrait Vessel*, 1991. Whiteware. 25 × 22 × 4¾ in. (63.5 × 55.9 × 12.1 cm). Arizona State University Art Museum, Gift of Anne and Sam Davis.

**Ralph Bacerra,** *Untitled Turquoise Bowl*, 2006. Ceramic. Height: 14½ in. (36.9 cm); diameter: 25 in. (63.5 cm).

## NOTES

Special thanks to Jo Lauria for her commentary on early drafts of this text and to Adrianna Spinozzi and Sequoia Miller for their helpfulness with technical questions.

1. Porcelain blanks—or undecorated glazed porcelain forms of vases, cups, and saucers but most commonly plates—were imported from France and Germany in large quantities for china painters.

2. Cynthia Brandimarte, "Somebody's Aunt and Nobody's Mother: The American China Painter and Her Work, 1870–1920," *Winterthur Portfolio* 23 (Winter 1988): 203–24. For more information on the history of china painting, see the bibliography at the end of this essay.

3. On the prevalence of modernist values in the academy as late as the 1970s, see Jamie Bennett's lecture "Traditions and Transformations: Working Locally" (1998), cited in Jeannine Falino, *Edge of the Sublime: Enamels by Jamie Bennett* (Brockton, MA: Fuller Craft Museum; New York: Hudson Hills, 2008), which presents his early perspective on pattern decoration. Bennett struggled with his attraction to decoration, which he was taught to consider as "cosmetic garnishing of a form or picture which was somehow lacking structure and therefore integrity."

4. Bacerra did not officially study with Otto Heino, Vivika's husband, but he considered both of them to be mentors. Otto may not have taught formally at Chouinard, but he worked alongside Vivika and gave demonstrations so that students could watch him work.

5. Quotations and recollections cited here are from the oral history interview with Ralph Bacerra, conducted by Frank Lloyd, April 7–19, 2004, Archives of American Art, Smithsonian Institution. The interviews were conducted at the artist's home in the Eagle Rock neighborhood of Los Angeles.

6. Ibid.

7. According to Bacerra, "Stoneware at that time was—or high-temperature firing was becoming very popular in all of the universities. And all the schools were building stoneware kilns or buying—[Paul] Soldner built his own at Claremont, and then Susan [Peterson] would have West Coast Kiln build them for her at SC [University of Southern California]." Ibid.

8. The artist continued to teach and demonstrate with stoneware and other materials in the classroom despite his personal focus on whiteware and porcelain. Whiteware is a low-fire earthenware that has been formulated with clay, silica, and feldspar so that it will vitrify and become impermeable to liquids; it is white or off-white.

9. He revisited the same countries during two additional trips in 1981 and 1982, adding the Philippines and Singapore to this list. Jo Lauria, telephone conversation with the author, February 2015.

10. John Coplans, "Abstract Expressionist Ceramics," in *Abstract Expressionist Ceramics* (Irvine: Art Gallery, University of California, 1966), 70.

11. Ron Nagle, oral history interview conducted by Bill Berkson, San Francisco, July 8–9, 2003, Archives of American Art, Smithsonian Institution.

12. Other artists working in low-fire included Fred Bauer, Margaret Ford, Erik Gronberg, and Peter VandenBerge.

13. Clement Greenberg, "Avant-garde and Kitsch," *Partisan Review* 6, no. 5 (1939): 34–49.

14. The power wielded by Greenberg, called the "Greenberg effect" by Caroline Jones, was pervasive. Caroline Jones, *Eyesight Alone: Clement Greenberg's Modernism and the Bureaucratization of the Senses* (Chicago: University of Chicago Press, 2005), 17–21. See also Kim Levin, "Farewell to Modernism," *Arts Magazine* 54 (October 1979): 90–92.

15. Judy Chicago, "World of the China Painter," in *Overglaze Imagery Cone 019-016*, ed. Dextra Frankel (Fullerton: Art Gallery, Visual Arts Center, California State University, 1977), 115–19. For a recent publication on *The Dinner Party*, see Jane Gerhard, *The Dinner Party: Judy Chicago and the Power of Popular Feminism, 1970–2007* (Athens: University of Georgia Press, 2013).

16. John Perreault, "The Heart of the Matter," in *Miriam Schapiro: A Retrospective, 1953–1980*, ed. Thalia Gouma-Peterson (Wooster, OH: College of Wooster, 1980), 40–42. See also Amy Goldin, "Pattern and Print," *Print Collector's Newsletter* 9 (March–April 1978): 10–13.

17. Hayden Herrera, "A Conversation with the Artist," in *Joyce Kozloff: Visionary Ornament*, by Patricia Johnston (Boston: Boston University Art Gallery, 1986), 29.

18. Illustrated in Johnston, *Joyce Kozloff*, 36–37.

19. A casual look through today's art publications demonstrates the multiplicity of artistic expressions in all mediums that include decorative elements as expressed in pattern and decoration.

20. Surviving stencils in the artist's studio confirm this technique. Jo Lauria, correspondence with the author, August 6, 2015.

21. See the essay by Hollis Goodall in this volume for an in-depth examination of Bacerra's fascination with East Asian ceramics.

22. Bacerra's retirement was prompted by the closure of the ceramics department when the school came under "conceptualist" influence. Garth Clark, "Ralph Bacerra 1938–2008," *Ceramics Monthly* 56 (February 2008): 48–50.

23. Susan Peterson, *The Craft and Art of Clay: A Complete Potter's Handbook*, 2nd ed. (London: Calmann & King, 1996), 200.

24. The Blue Four artists were represented by their patron the German dealer and artist Galka Scheyer (1889–1945), whose collection was given to the Pasadena Art Museum (now the Norton Simon Museum) in 1953.

25. Bacerra, oral history interview.

26. Ibid.

## FURTHER READING

**Archives of American Art, Smithsonian Institution.** Oral history interview with Ralph Bacerra, conducted by Frank Lloyd, April 7–19, 2004.

**Denker, Ellen Paul.** "The Grammar of Nature: Arts and Crafts China Painting." In *The Substance of Style: Perspectives on the American Arts and Crafts Movement*, edited by Bert Denker, 281–300. Winterthur, DE: Henry Francis du Pont Winterthur Museum, 1996.

———. "Hot Bodies, Cool Colors: American China Painting in Two Centuries." In *Ceramics in America 2014*, edited by Robert Hunter, 147–68. Milwaukee: Chipstone Foundation, 2014.

**Frankel, Dextra, ed.** *Overglaze Imagery Cone 019-016*. Fullerton: Art Gallery, Visual Arts Center, California State University, 1977.

**Lewing, Paul.** *China Paint and Overglaze*. Westerville, OH: American Ceramic Society, 2007.

**Ralph Bacerra**, *Untitled Bowl*, 2008. Ceramic. Height: 18½
in. (45.7 cm); diameter: 22 in. (55.9 cm). Collection of
Douglas Moreland.

# Nefertiti Series | 1972-74    JO LAURIA

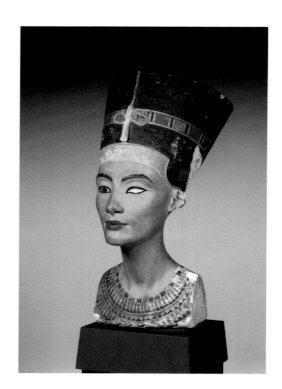

Dazzling artifacts from the tomb of Tutankhamun were first seen in the United States in the exhibition *Tutankhamun Treasures*, which toured from 1961 to 1966, stopping at the Los Angeles County Museum of Art (LACMA) toward the end of its travels. Like many Americans, Bacerra fell under the spell of the precious and mysterious objects excavated from the tomb of the Egyptian "boy king." According to his former student Peter Shire, Bacerra fixated on the painted limestone bust of Queen Nefertiti when he saw the sculpture (left), on view at LACMA. He told Shire that he coveted the queen's portrait—wanting a Nefertiti of his own— citing the unequaled beauty and elegance of this regal bust. Knowing that he would never possess the object of his desire, Bacerra embarked on making his own versions of Nefertiti, using clay and glaze rather than limestone and paint.

Bacerra's Nefertiti sculptures were far afield of the ancient Egyptian model. Eschewing realism for abstraction, he incisively interpreted the pose, scale, and silhouette of the queen but loosely translated the contours of the sculpture into a fluid, expressive line that described stacking volumes rather than defined body parts. In place of realistic depictions of facial features and clothing, Bacerra created imaginative embellishments of colorful geometric and organic designs that fluidly embrace the sculptures. The artist worked on the series for two years—from 1972 to 1974—and with every new variation, he challenged himself to explore color and texture combinations, repetition of shapes and lines, the interplay of positive and negative space, and the melding of surface decoration with form. Bacerra's versions of Nefertiti may stretch the definition of portraiture, but sculpturally each is as powerful, commanding, and seductive as the awe-inspiring Egyptian original.

Bust of Queen Nefertiti. New Kingdom, Dynasty 18, c. 1340 BC. Limestone, gypsum, crystal, wax. Height: 19.7 in. (50 cm). Aegyptisches Museum und Papyrussammlung, Berlin.

**Ralph Bacerra**, *Nefertiti*, c. 1972. Ceramic. 22 × 7½ × 7 in. (55.9 × 19.1 × 17.8 cm). Collection of Ava Shire.

**Ralph Bacerra**, *Nefertiti*, c. 1972–74. Ceramic. 23 × 7½ × 6 in. (58.4 × 19.1 × 15.2 cm). Private collection.

Opposite: **Ralph Bacerra**, Untitled, 2002. Ceramic. Height: 23½ in. (59.7 cm); diameter: 8 in. (20.3 cm). Collection of Dr. and Mrs. Terasaki.

Above: **Ralph Bacerra**, *Untitled Lidded Vessel*, 1998. Earthenware. 29 × 17½ × 16 in. (73.7 × 44.5 × 40.6 cm). Collection of David and Julianne Armstrong, Promised gift to the American Museum of Ceramic Art.

# Ralph Bacerra and Ceramic Forms of East Asia

HOLLIS GOODALL

Ralph Bacerra had an abiding fascination with the ceramics of East Asia and Iran. He fostered this interest, which was initially stimulated when he attended a workshop given by the *mingei* (folk art) movement potter Shōji Hamada in 1963, through reading and repeated study trips to the Asian Art Museum of San Francisco, the Los Angeles County Museum of Art, and the Pacific Asia Museum in Pasadena. In the 1960s and early 1970s, when he pursued these studies, the Asian Art Museum of San Francisco was a subsection of the M. H. de Young Memorial Museum in Golden Gate Park, and it featured a "Treasure Wall" of ceramics from China, including monochrome vases, vessels with underglaze blue designs and some with overglaze enamels, and Longquan wares with green glazes and designs in biscuit reserve (p. 31). One can see the influence of the latter type in Bacerra's underglaze blue vessels with *tenmoku* brown glaze rims, which reveal a similar aesthetic of contrast.

The Japanese galleries at the same museum also boasted an excellent display of ceramics, thanks to the shared interests of the museum's patron Avery Brundage and its curator of Japanese art, Yoshiko Kakudo. Of most significance to Bacerra was Oribe stoneware with black, green, and orange glazes showing informal drawings of local scenery and overglaze enamel on porcelain wares such as seventeenth-century Old Kutani (Kokutani) and nineteenth-century Kutani revival ceramics, which shared a color palette of green, indigo, purple, and yellow, sometimes including red. Kokutani wares were made during the mid- to late seventeenth century in Arita, the porcelain-producing

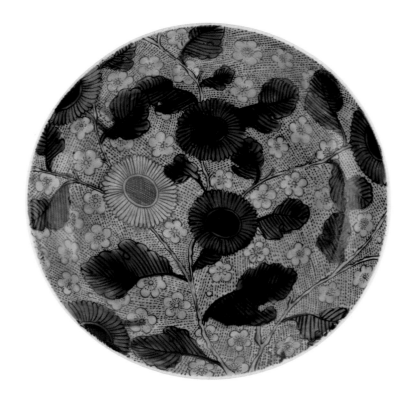

Left: **Ralph Bacerra**, *Cloud Vessel*, 2000. Porcelain. 22 × 14½ × 6 in. (55.9 × 36.8 × 15.2 cm). Collection of Paul and Sharon Dauer.

Above: *Plate*, Japan, c. 1650–60. Arita ware, Kokutani style; porcelain with overglaze enamels. Height: 2⅜ in. (6 cm); diameter: 13¾ in. (34.9 cm). Los Angeles County Museum of Art; Purchased with funds provided by the Art Museum Council, AC1992.110.1.

center in northern Kyushu, which is the westernmost of the main Japanese islands. Kokutani ceramics fall into two main categories. The earlier feature Chinese-style designs of diaper patterning—repeat patterning in areas of open surface—interrupted by cartouches and a central roundel with either a bird and flower or a figure in a landscape motif. The later type, called *aode*, has an overall design of inventively composed large motifs drawn from textile designs, often featuring large flowers, birds, fishing nets, or trees on a dense, overall background scheme of simplified flowers, waves, or geometric designs (p. 51).

In his mixing of large floral and small geometric designs, Bacerra showed his knowledge of both Kokutani types. Kokutani was made at the behest of the wealthiest feudal lords in Japan after the shogun, the Maeda clan, and was produced as giftware to be given to other feudal lords or samurai and for export to South Asia. Revival Kutani ware of the nineteenth century, derived from Kokutani in color and pattern but made in present-day Ishikawa Prefecture, home territory of the Maeda clan, differs from the original type in its cleaner, more regularized design and cooler overall tone. There is also a category of revival Kutani ware drawn from Kyoto precedents that has fine-line red overglaze with gold highlights, and another type, influenced by Imari ware, is preponderantly red with delicate details. Bacerra would have had much more access to this revival type, due to the specialized use of the earlier Kokutani wares and because later Kutani wares were sold commercially in larger numbers. A plate with illusionistic checkered columns (opposite) carries a modernized version of the Kutani palette, using manganese and copper glazes to recall the darker purples and greens of Kutani.

Another kiln organized by feudal lords to produce giftware was that for the Nabeshima lords, and Bacerra often mentioned these highly refined porcelains as a central inspiration for him (below). Like those on *aode* Kokutani wares, designs on many Nabeshima ceramics were drawn from woodblock-printed books illustrating kimono designs, and in the seventeenth and early eighteenth centuries they tended to

feature large patterns composed of magnified motifs such as flowers, fruits, radishes, fans, tassels, fishing nets, boats, or anything with a dynamic shape, often asymmetrically placed against a blank white or celadon ground. Nabeshima ware also features a high foot and a triad of running underglaze blue floral motifs on the undersides of plates and bowls. These features are found on the reverse of some of

Above: *Dish with Daffodil and Wave Design*, Japan, Edo period (1615–1868), 1700–1750. Nabeshima ware; porcelain with underglaze blue and overglaze red, yellow, and green enamels. Height: 1¾ in. (4.5 cm); diameter: 5⅞ in. (14.9 cm). Los Angeles County Museum of Art; Gift of Leslie Prince Salzman, M.2007.8.

Right: **Ralph Bacerra**, *Untitled Platter*, 1988. Earthenware with underglaze, glaze, and overglaze painting. 3½ × 24 × 24 in. (8.9 × 61 × 61 cm). Collection of Bronya and Andy Galef.

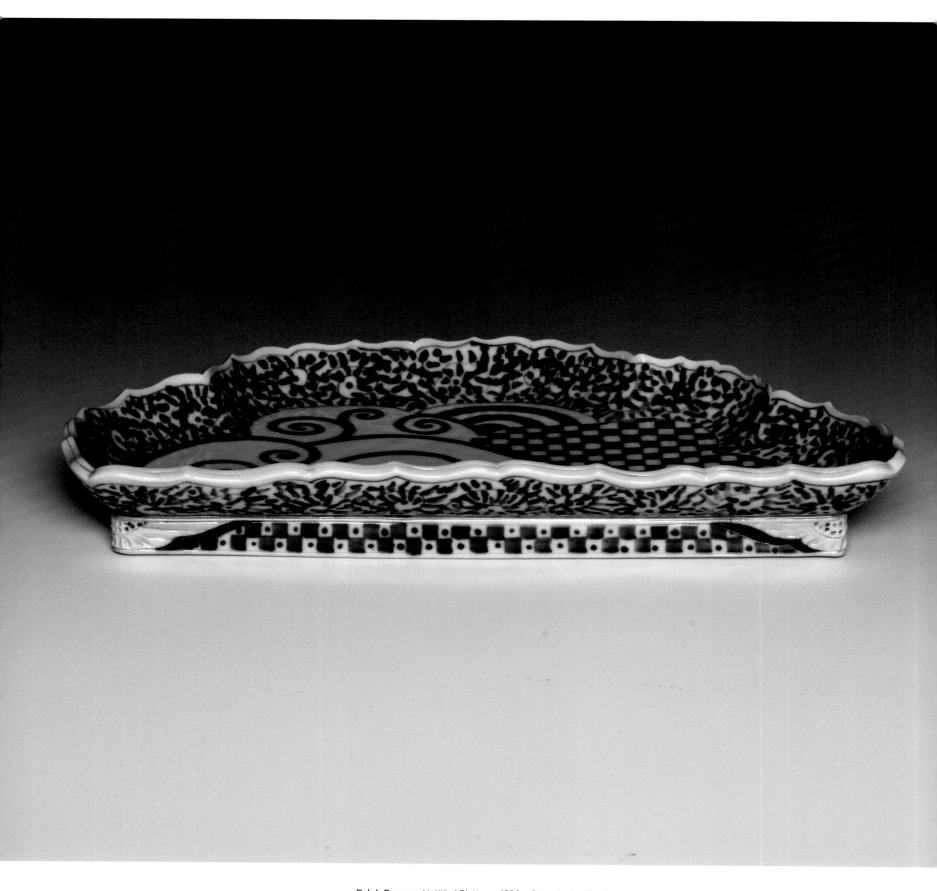

**Ralph Bacerra**, *Untitled Platter*, c. 1980s. Ceramic. 2 × 12 × 7
in. (5.1 × 30.5 × 17.8 cm).

Bacerra's platter and bowl forms as well (opposite). A taste for textile motifs is also evident in his work, as he incorporated wave patterns, flowers, vines, geometric, and other repeating designs between and around his primary motifs, often triangles and squares, clouds, or birds.[1]

Bacerra was particularly fond of two more overglaze enamel types, both made in Arita. One is known as Imari ware for the harbor at Imari, from which vast quantities of these ceramics were shipped abroad (top right). The other, overglaze enamels of the Kakiemon type (below right), lighter in palette than Imari ware, featured painting of the type practiced by the official Kano school, which catered to the shogunate and samurai class, and the Tosa school, patronized by the imperial court and nobility. Colors on these porcelains were azure, pale yellow, and green, with small amounts of red or orange, only the latter two being opaque and the rest translucent. The string-like motifs that Bacerra would use to draw one's eye around his vessels (p. 53) are reminiscent of the elegant branch and tendril designs used for the same purpose on Kakiemon wares. Kakiemon pieces often sported a brown edge, a feature echoed in the brown-rimmed ceramics created by Bacerra.

Imari ware was a product of kilns in the same area of Arita as Kakiemon, but its color scheme was much stronger in its use of red, blue, silver, and gold, the brilliant red and deep blue attracting Bacerra to these porcelains above all others. Full-color Imari wares with red and metallic overglazes (as opposed to the blue-and-white Imari examples) are referred to as *nishikide*, or brocade ware, and his midcareer works featuring a *horror vacui* aesthetic convey the impression of brocaded patterns. Bacerra's attraction to Imari ware is revealed

Above: *Large Basin*, Japan, Meiji period (1868–1912). Fukagawa ware; porcelain with overglaze enamels and gold. 7³⁄₁₆ × 19½ × 19⁵⁄₁₆ in. (18.2 × 49.5 × 49 cm). Los Angeles County Museum of Art; The Louis R. and Deborah Mosbrooker Bequest, M.2001.123.2.

Below: *Plate*, Japan, Edo period (1615–1868), c. 1660–90. Arita ware, Kakiemon style; porcelain with overglaze decoration. Diameter: 12½ in. (31.7 cm). Los Angeles County Museum of Art; Ernest Larsen Blank Memorial Fund, 62.14.2.

in a cloud-shaped box (above) and a platter (right), which display the red, blue, and metallic palette. The cloud-shaped box is of demilune form, recalling an Imari shape called a "bow shoreline," which, like this box, has a straight side and a side that bows out, the bowed side embellished with undulating curves. Such Imari plates often featured a cloud-shaped foot.

Imari wares of the eighteenth century and later versions from the late nineteenth and early twentieth centuries have designs based on early Qing dynasty (1644–1911) Chinese ceramics, some with a flower petal scheme in which each petal along the rim holds subsidiary motifs and the central roundel of the "flower" in the middle of the plate is filled by a pictorial motif. Alternatively, diaper or scrolling patterns

**Ralph Bacerra**, *Untitled Lidded Box*, n.d. Ceramic. 3½ × 11 × 6 in. (8.9 × 27.9 × 15.2 cm). Collection of Ted Rowland.

**Ralph Bacerra**, *Untitled Platter*, 2007. Ceramic. Height:
4 in. (10.2 cm); diameter: 28¼ in. (71.8 cm). Collection of
David and Julianne Armstrong.

with symmetrically placed cartouches run along the rim, and again a picture anchors the center of the plate. The symmetrical regularity of these painting schemes is not found in Bacerra's work, though there, as in Imari ware, geometric or organic forms can act as background diaper patterns to set off larger motifs.

Bacerra acquired numerous examples of both Chinese and Japanese underglaze blue wares and Imari porcelains at antique stores in North America and in the course of his several trips to East Asia. He traveled to Japan, Taiwan (where he was particularly fond of the National Palace Museum), Hong Kong, and South Korea several times in the 1980s,

frequently for business having to do with Fasar stove tops, for which he designed and made tile inserts (below). In Japan, Bacerra was able to visit ceramics sites, museums, and temples, gleaning stimulus from all that he saw but also accumulating brushes, tools, and overglaze enamels with which to experiment. He brought blue-and-white wares and overglaze Imari porcelains, as well as equipment, back to Otis Art Institute, and over subsequent years he worked with students to reverse-engineer the decorating techniques that they could see close-up on the plates and vessels that he provided. The lower-temperature firing of these enamels was a particular challenge for the students, as were the recipes for glazes, which he demanded that they find through experimentation.[2] Bacerra also spoke to his students about positive and negative space on Imari, Kutani, and Nabeshima wares, as well as dark and light tones, superior techniques in handling detail, and engineering of designs using foreground and background motifs while noting their relation to the form. His creative response to these issues is well illustrated by a footed and lidded vessel with celadon and blue and

Above: From 1971 to 1975 Bacerra designed and made tiles for Fasar ceramic cooktops. This 12-by-12-inch tile displaying a simple floral motif outlined against a rich iron-saturate glaze was one of his more popular designs.

Above, top: **Ralph Bacerra**, *Untitled Covered Vessel*, c. 1980s. Porcelain. Height: 12 in. (30.5 cm); diameter: 15 in. (38.1 cm).

Right: **Ralph Bacerra**, *Untitled Animal Form*, c. 1976. Ceramic. 33 × 41¼ × 10 in. (83.8 × 104.8 × 25.4 cm). Collection of Forrest L. Merrill.

with celadon and blue and white glazes (left). In his own work he would add emphasis to designs by using some overglaze enamels with enough body that they would be raised above the surface, thus surpassing the embellishments of his original models, which mostly clung to their surfaces.[3]

In addition to focusing on surface decoration, Bacerra also wished his students to understand sculptural structure in clay. From a deaccession sale at the Los Angeles County Museum of Art around 1965, he purchased Chinese Tang dynasty–style animals partly for their striking presence but also to analyze how these figures were applied to their bases and what kind of substructure kept them aloft. Years later, in 1991, he was able to accompany students to a special exhibition titled *Quest for Eternity: Chinese Ceramic Sculptures from the People's Republic of China* at the Los Angeles County Museum of Art, where they were treated to a great variety of figural sculptures fresh from archaeological digs. Drawing on his early figures in homage to the Tang works prepared Bacerra to do a new set of figural sculptures, such as his untitled animal form from around 1976 (below), and the later exposure to *Quest*

*for Eternity* resulted in an untitled female figure in 1994 (p. 86), which he referred to as "Tang type." This approach is also reflected in his contemporaneous work with wood shapes.[4]

Bacerra's interest in Japanese ceramics was not confined to premodern materials. He also had a particular appreciation for the work of Kenkichi Tomimoto, who had started out as a member of the *mingei* movement along with Hamada but moved to overglaze enameling on porcelain at midcentury. Tomimoto is considered among ceramists and design curators in Japan to be the foremost overglaze enamel design innovator and top porcelain decorator of the twentieth century in that country. He was a close lifelong friend of Bernard Leach, and they made

a pact to "never make patterns from patterns," looking always to forms in nature and abstracting from there. Tomimoto's use of quatrefoil-form flowers and ferns is reflected in the tetrahedrons or triangles that appear on works by Bacerra such as his lidded vessel from 2001 (opposite). The overall massing of these decorative forms creates a dizzying effect in the work of both artists, which Bacerra emphasized by having his triangles lift off from and distort the surface.

On the same lidded vessel from 2001, the squared lid, neck, base, and plinth are all similar in form to carved square or rectangular scholar's desk objects or ceremonial wares of the Korean Goryeo (918–1392) and Joseon dynasties (1392–1910), such as brush holders, water droppers, or incense burners. Those would tend to be pierced with geometric motifs, which Bacerra elaborated here into designs that recall art deco. A cloud-form vessel from 1997 features a crackled white glaze that resembles that of Chinese Song dynasty *guan* or *ge* wares, though it is a light form of celadon (p. 62). The glaze of another cloud vessel from the same year resembles the celadon preponderant in the Goryeo dynasty in Korea (p. 63). This glaze is more reminiscent of Korean celadons than of Chinese or Japanese versions because of its gray-green hue, which gets its specific color from the amount of iron in the clay, along with manganese and quartz in the glaze. The cloud form may reflect Bacerra's interest in motifs associated with spirituality in Asian cultures. The main Daoist temple in China is named the White Cloud Temple. Though we do not know whether he was aware of this, it does illustrate the association in East Asia of clouds with spirituality, and he mentioned being struck by Chinese paintings on spiritual

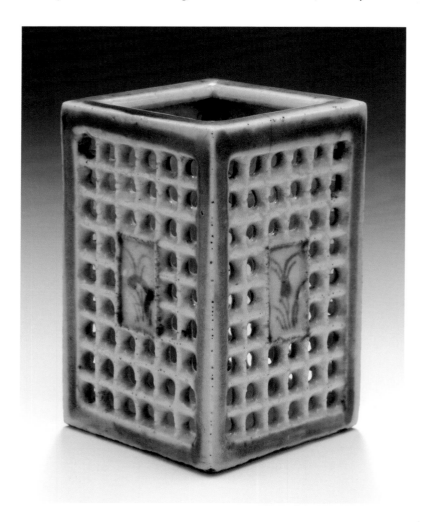

*Brush Holder*, Korea, Joseon dynasty (1392–1910), 18th century. Slab-built and pierced porcelain with cobalt and copper painted decoration under clear glaze. 3½ × 2¼ × 2¼ in. (8.9 × 5.7 × 5.7 cm). Los Angeles County Museum of Art; Gift of Dr. Michael Moon Ki Chang and family.

**Ralph Bacerra**, *Untitled Lidded Vessel*, 2001. Earthenware. 32 × 16 × 9½ in. (81.3 × 40.6 × 24.1 cm).

**Ralph Bacerra**, *Untitled Cloud Vessel*, 1997. Porcelain. 20 × 13 × 5 in. (50.8 × 33 × 12.7 cm). Private collection.

**Ralph Bacerra**, *Untitled Cloud Vessel*, 1997. Porcelain. 20½ × 13 × 6 in. (52.1 × 33 × 15.2 cm). Collection of Saul E. Levi.

interest in roof tiles during trips to Japan on which she accompanied him in the early 1980s.[6] Japanese roof tiles, especially those on temples, are often adorned with cloud motifs, which evoke proximity to heaven; yin-yang symbols, representing the dark and light forces of existence; or *mitsutomoe*, the three-comma symbol of the "three divisions" in Shinto—humankind, earth, and sky. Bacerra's memories of these roof tiles seem to have stayed with him as he proceeded into his cloud vessel phase in the late 1990s.

Although he did not travel to Iran, Persian art was also a great inspiration to Bacerra. It is likely that he saw objects that stimulated his interest in the collections of the Los Angeles County Museum of Art, such as blue fritware vessels from Iran dated to the thirteenth century. These underglaze-painted wares with a blue glaze are reflected in Bacerra's monumental vessels using the same hues. He claimed to have been interested in Iznik pottery with red, blue, and green overglaze enamels, also fritware, and Persian miniature painting, which features a flattened perspective and mix of mineral pigments with metallic leaf that must certainly have spoken to his taste for intensely decorated surfaces.

Bacerra, although deeply interested in the ceramics of East Asia, declared himself to be a purely American artist. The forms and techniques of Asian ceramics that he absorbed through his studies were in subsequent years subsumed into his distinctive personal style.

## NOTES

1. According to Bacerra's student and travel companion Lin Werner, he was particularly drawn to textiles during his excursions with her to Japan (conversation with the author, September 2014). Further evidence of his fascination with textile patterns was provided by his student Joan Takayama-Ogawa, who witnessed him referring to a book on textile patterns while at work in his studio (conversation with the author, August 2014). Such a book found in Bacerra's library is Clarence P. Hornung's *Allover Patterns for Designers and Craftsmen* (New York: Dover, 1975), which in its introduction claims to have drawn mainly from Japanese decorative arts. I am grateful to Jo Lauria for providing this reference.
2. In this respect Bacerra was following in the footsteps of his teacher and mentor Vivika Heino. See the oral history interview with Bacerra conducted by Frank Lloyd, April 7–19, 2004, Archives of American Art, Smithsonian Institution.
3. I am grateful to Joan Takayama-Ogawa for the information about Bacerra's teaching methods that she shared in conversations in August 2014.
4. Oral history interview with Bacerra conducted by Frank Lloyd.
5. Peter Clothier, "Ralph Bacerra Needs Time to Play," *American Ceramics* 13, no. 1 (1999): 24.
6. Lin Werner, conversation with the author, September 2014.

## FURTHER READING

**Archives of American Art, Smithsonian Institution.** Oral history interview with Ralph Bacerra, conducted by Frank Lloyd, April 7–19, 2004.
**Fitski, Menno, and Harriet Impey.** *Kakiemon Porcelain: A Handbook.* Leiden: Leiden University Press; Amsterdam: Rijksmuseum, 2011.
**Impey, Oliver R.** *The Early Porcelain Kilns of Japan: Arita in the First Half of the Seventeenth Century.* Oxford: Clarendon; New York: Oxford University Press, 1996.
**Nakagawa, Sensaku.** *Kutani Ware.* Tokyo: Kodansha International, 1979.

**Ralph Bacerra**, *Double Portrait*, 1996. Porcelain. Height: 9 in. (22.9 cm); diameter: 15 in. (38.1 cm). Private collection.

## Tang Horse Series | 1976    JO LAURIA

Throughout his career Bacerra maintained an unwavering interest in Asian ceramics. When a pair of Chinese ceramic horses in the Tang dynasty style was offered as part of a deacquisition sale by the Los Angeles County Museum of Art in the mid-1960s, he was quick to purchase the set. The prized "Tang" horses were prominently displayed as decorative focal points in his Pasadena home, and they served an additional purpose: as study models. Ken Deavers—founder of the American Hand gallery in Washington, DC, and a dealer of Bacerra's work as early as 1967—remembers discussing the acquisition of the horses with the artist. As Deavers recalls, Bacerra was captivated by the structural mechanics of the sculptures: the balance, distribution of weight, and stability of the hefty equine bodies supported on four slender legs, each perched on an edge of a thin rectangular base. Deavers sensed that Bacerra found in the model of the Tang horse a challenge to his craftsmanship and was determined to reverse-engineer the sculpture to construct his own version.

So in 1976 Bacerra began building a series of four-legged animal-like sculptures set on narrow rectangular platform bases. Whereas the Chinese versions of the Tang horse were made by molding clay over a prefabricated form, Bacerra chose to hand-build each sculpture individually, thus assuring the uniqueness of every presentation. Further, he added complexity to the mechanics of his animal forms by engineering their elongated bodies to be held aloft on four gangly legs—twisted, bent, and arranged in dynamic, animated poses that suggest that the animal was capable of leaping off its base at any moment. And in his inimitable style, Bacerra decorated the surfaces with bold patterns of high-key glazes and metallic lusters, creating a design that enhanced and defined the volume, shape, and silhouette. He delighted in populating the landscape around his studio in Eagle Rock with the wildly inventive animal sculptures, improvising his own personal menagerie.

A pair of Bacerra's untitled animal forms are displayed in the exhibition, positioned at the gallery entrance to welcome and beguile visitors.

*Funerary Sculpture of a Horse*, Middle Tang dynasty, c. 700–800. Molded earthenware with molded, applied, and incised decoration and polychrome (*sancai*) glaze. 29½ × 29⅞ × 10⅛ in. (74.9 × 75.9 × 25.7 cm). Los Angeles County Museum of Art, Gift of Nasli M. Heeramaneck.

Ralph Bacerra with his untitled animal forms in the yard of his Eagle Rock home.

**Ralph Bacerra**, *Untitled Animal Form*, c. 1976. Ceramic. 34 ¾ × 35 ⅞ × 16 ⅝ in. (88.3 × 91.1 × 42.2 cm). Collection of Forrest L. Merrill.

Overleaf, left: **Ralph Bacerra**, Untitled, 2002. Ceramic. Height: 29 in. (73.7 cm); diameter: 14 in. (35.6 cm). Collection of Lois and Robert Boardman.

Overleaf, right: **Ralph Bacerra**, Untitled, 2003. Whiteware. 29 × 12 × 6 in. (73.7 × 30.5 × 15.2 cm). Collection of David and Julianne Armstrong.

**Ralph Bacerra.** *Teapot*, 1989. Ceramic. 17 × 12 × 8½ in. (43.2 × 30.5 × 21.6 cm). Collection of Lucille H. Epstein.

Right: Ralph Bacerra teaching at Chouinard Art Institute, c. 1970. On the blackboard behind him are notes from his Glaze Technology class.

# Crossroads in Clay at Chouinard and Otis

## THE RALPH BACERRA YEARS

CHRISTY JOHNSON

Teaching was an important aspect of Ralph Bacerra's practice. He spent two periods of time teaching in Los Angeles. From 1963 to 1971 he taught at Chouinard Art Institute, and in 1982 he began teaching at what was then known as Otis Art Institute of Parsons School of Design, becoming head of the ceramics department the following year and continuing to teach there until 1996.[1] A significant number of his students have risen to prominence, and many are currently ceramics instructors. Concurrently with the presentation of *Exquisite Beauty: The Ceramics of Ralph Bacerra* at Otis's Ben Maltz Gallery, *Crossroads in Clay at Chouinard and Otis: The Ralph Bacerra Years* will be on view at the Vincent Price Art Museum at East Los Angeles College.[2] *Crossroads in Clay* offers an opportunity to consider the diverse ceramic works created by the inheritors of Bacerra's knowledge of the medium and to consider how his influence is manifested in their practices.

Of his influence on his students, Bacerra said, "It isn't that I've influenced them to do what I do. I don't know of one artist in the field today that has gotten either his bachelor's or master's from me that does work that I do."[3] Intentionally or not, however, teachers do influence their students. European old masters honed the skills of their apprentices by requiring them to make copies of their mentor's work. But

interpreting influence as merely an aesthetic phenomenon—in which an artist reflects on another artist's work, is inspired by it, or borrows elements of it—limits the significance of the concept.

Influence is a complicated topic because it covers virtually everything that touches our lives. Consider influence as it pertained to Bacerra's own artistic life. His love of hard-edge design most likely stemmed from his initial studies in graphic design at Chouinard. After he switched to ceramics, his work took on characteristics of the pottery made by his teacher Vivika Heino and her husband, Otto (below). Visits to the Pasadena Art Museum nurtured his admiration for the artists Lyonel Feininger, Vassily Kandinsky, Paul Klee, and especially M. C. Escher.[4] Later, when Bacerra became enamored of Japanese design, his work shadowed an Asian aesthetic.

Bacerra was only twenty-five when he began teaching at Chouinard. Suki Diamond says, "He was our teacher but not very much older than us; we tested him."[5] Don Pilcher describes Bacerra's early focus: "He was still a stoneware potter in something of the Chouinard tradition, an organic, fluid kind of stuff, but not in the Peter Voulkos way."[6]

As a teacher Bacerra influenced his students in tangible ways. He demonstrated ceramic construction methods—wheel throwing, hand building, and slip casting—and expected his students to master them. He expected them to know the technical aspects of the craft—ceramic tools, glaze formulation, and firing—and he exposed students to various decorative techniques, including glaze application and brushwork. Originally the ceramics studio at Chouinard focused on stoneware clay, but subsequently a wider variety of materials were available: porcelain, earthenware, colored underglazes, china paint, and lusters.[7] Sharon Jeniye recalls that students at Chouinard spent several months each year making work for a popular public sale that subsidized scholarships. This effort simulated a production studio experience and provided valuable practice in basic skills.[8]

Three large plates by Juanita Jimenez, Jun Kaneko, and Mineo Mizuno are representative of Chouinard student work of the 1960s. The first two typify two styles of midcentury stoneware. Jimenez incorporates Japanese-style brushwork, popularized by the *mingei* (folk art) movement, brought to the United States by Shōji Hamada. Kaneko's plate displays affinities with abstract expressionism but shows little of the preciseness of his later larger-than-life sculptures from his Dango series. Mizuno's porcelain platter, reflecting his Japanese heritage

**Ralph Bacerra**, *Untitled Vessel*, c. 1958–61. Stoneware. Height: 15 in. (38.1 cm); diameter: 13 in. (33 cm). Photograph from Bacerra's portfolio documenting his student work at Chouinard. The scale and shape of this vessel and the glaze treatment show the influence of Vivika Heino.

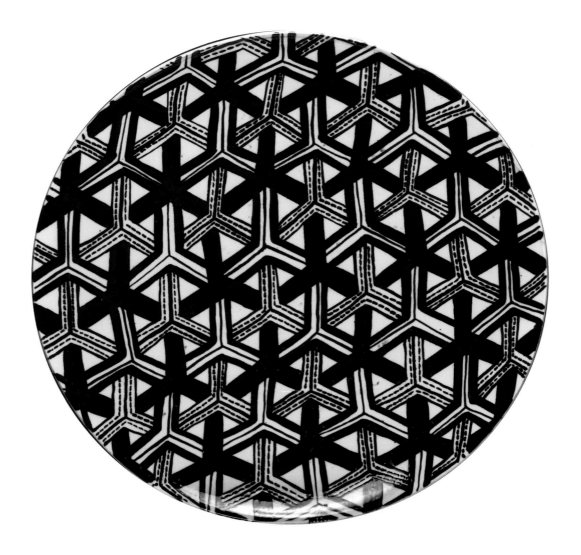

(above), exhibits a complex interwoven design known as a tortoiseshell pattern. Kaneko and Mizuno were among many international students, mainly Asian, who were attracted to Bacerra because they had heard of his reputation for superb craftsmanship and extraordinary skills, especially in traditional Asian techniques.[9]

The work of two other Chouinard students reflects Asian models. Jeniye painted plates with underglaze patterns, akin to modern interpretations of kimono fabric design. Lin Werner recalls, "Inspired by a class in Chinese painting, I began to paint cobalt oxide on my work in porcelain."[10] Her work morphed into a whimsical series of imaginary rabbits superimposed against calligraphic Asian landscapes. Werner's originals eventually led to a commercial project destined for the giftware market.

Elsa Rady began classes at Chouinard with Bacerra when she was just sixteen years old. Her forms were uncomplicated (p. 74, left), and her use of porcelain provided an ideal surface for presenting the

**Mineo Mizuno** (Japan, b. 1944), *Untitled Platter*, 1969. Porcelain. Height: 3½ in. (8.9 cm); diameter: 30 in. (76.2 cm). Scripps College, Fred and Mary Marer Collection.

beauty of Korean, Chinese, and Japanese traditional glazes. Likewise, Don Pilcher, also one of Bacerra's earliest students, capitalized on these time-honored elegant finishes. His recent work includes small, irregular globular forms covered with gold luster (a favorite Bacerra embellishment).

Bacerra shaped his students' critical faculties by holding weekly evaluations, asking such questions as "Is this piece functional?" "Is it beautiful?" and "What makes it work?" Discussions of wheel-thrown work considered such elements as the lip, the flange, or the lift of a

bowl.[11] Student opinions on the effectiveness of these critiques vary. Leonard Skuro notes that Bacerra's reviews were tough but that in a sense this harshness was an act of caring.[12]

All agree that Bacerra's optimum influence occurred through demos or through class assignments that he too would complete. Skuro adds, "Bacerra was a powerful force. It would have been hard to sit next to him, to see his private process day after day after day, and not realize the gift."[13] Sharing was a key element of the class experience. As part of the natural camaraderie of working alongside one another,

**Elsa Rady** (United States, 1943–2011), *Untitled Bottle*, c. 1970s. Porcelain. Height: 4½ in. (11.4 cm); diameter: 5¼ in. (13.3 cm). American Museum of Ceramic Art, Gift of James W. and Jackie Voell.

**Harry Berman** (United States, b. 1948), *Large Zoomorphic Forms*, c. 1969–70. Stoneware. Approx. 20 to 25 forms, ranging from 36 in. (91.4 cm) to 96 in. (243.8 cm) high. Courtesy of the artist.

influences traveled in all directions, from teacher to student, from student to student, and even from student to teacher. "We fed him as much as he fed us," comments Jimenez.[14]

Beyond the vessel format, Bacerra and his students addressed form, creating hollow, asymmetrical sculptures, hand built or assembled from a combination of wheel, coil, and slab sections. Harry Berman cites the English sculptor Henry Moore as the stimulus for his sculpture (below), but according to Bonnie Ikemura, large constructions were in vogue, and many ceramists followed the trend. She says,

"The stuff I was doing my senior year was real derivative. Development wise, Bacerra's forms were far away from what I was doing."[15] Among Bacerra's oversize works is a trio of mound- and obelisk-like earthenware forms that were shown in the Pasadena Art Museum's California Design Ten (1968; p. 94, fig. 21) and three freestanding anthropomorphic figures titled *Ibo*, *Candado*, and *Caribe*, included in California Design Eleven (1971; see p. 95, fig. 23).[16] A similar piece is documented in his photo archives.

Former Otis student Tetsuji Aono credits a much later series of Bacerra's figurative works, from 1994, as providing inspiration for his animal and human figures in clay. Aono's untitled giraffe figure (above) recalls one of Bacerra's class assignments: to include three sections—a base, a central shape, and a top—all in one piece. Aono's use of Swiss cheese–like holes has parallels with some of the pierced work in Bacerra's pieces.

As to intangible influence, all former students interviewed mentioned Bacerra's dedicated work ethic. They referred to his craftsmanship as impeccable. They saw his passion for ceramics but also witnessed a similar intense dedication to cooking, gardening, and travel. He had high expectations of himself and likewise of his students, but he was also generous and giving, providing technical assistance, helping with research, and sharing glaze formulas. Adrian Saxe recalls, "Ralph was interested in everything, and he brought it to our attention. So we went and visited shows, or [the artist] Beatrice Wood, or we would look at historic work, and he was knowledgeable enough to throw light on it. And he would let us bring it into our own practices."[17]

Peter Shire, who graduated from Chouinard in 1970, wanted to be a studio potter. He studied under Bacerra, but when he finally found his own ceramic voice, there seemed to be no commonality between his work and his teacher's other than a proclivity for geometric form and design (oppose, top). Shire's slab-built work transcends the traditions of pottery, but he still referenced Bacerra's pronouncements in an interview, "And what I strive for in my work. . . . The key element of making a pot is, A, volume. In short, the space that's contained or what isn't there, you know, the void inside the pot that creates it. And the other is that . . . it lifts, right? You don't want it sagging on the table."[18]

Bacerra left Chouinard in 1971, when it officially closed its Grand View campus. After ten years of commercial ceramic assignments, he returned to teaching, this time at Otis. Some of his classes there were entirely about process; others were strictly devoted to glaze formulation, a rarely offered subject. Bacerra required students to make hundreds of test tiles and small-scale pots on which to test different glaze recipes: traditional high-fired celadons, *tenmoku* glazes, ash glazes, and copper reds, as well as low-fire glaze combinations that ranged from

Above: **Tetsuji Aono** (Japan, b. 1969), *Untitled (giraffe)*, 2009. Ceramic. 65 × 36 × 18 in. (165.1 × 91.4 × 45.7 cm). Courtesy of the artist and L2 Kontemporary, Los Angeles.

Opposite, top: **Peter Shire** (United States, b. 1947), *Cubist Steam*, 1980. Ceramic. 8¾ × 19 × 8 in. (22.2 × 48.3 × 20.3 cm). Courtesy of the artist.

matte to glossy. One of his favorites, an "alligator skin" crawl glaze, appeared on some of his low-fire sculptures and on the base sections of his imaginative teapots. The formula, designed to separate much like the mud of a dry lake bed, originated with Otto Heino.[19] Bacerra passed on this formula to his student Kevin A. Myers, who used it for a large-scale installation exhibited in 2010 in *The Story of O: Graduate Fine Arts 1989–2009* at the Ben Maltz Gallery at Otis (right).[20] Another former Otis student, Marc Hoar, employs a high-fire version of the same glaze in his recent work.

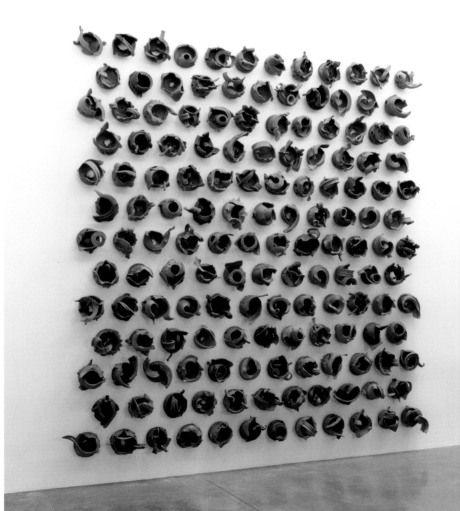

Right: **Kevin A. Myers** (United States, b. 1955), *Red Mural # 150*, 2010. Earthenware. 144 × 144 × 10 in. (365.8 × 365.8 × 25.4 cm). Courtesy of the artist.

James Haggerty has made glaze technology his life's work (above). Even while in high school, he was intrigued by the work of the famed potters Gertrud and Otto Natzler, whose cratered glazes took center stage for three decades (1940s through 1960s) and by Beatrice Wood's "Persian lusters," achieved by a strike reduction technique. Demonstrating his commitment to learning the complexities of glaze calculation at Otis, Haggerty's is the second most frequently listed name in Bacerra's roll books, appearing eleven times.[21] Today Haggerty's practice of mixing and testing approximately forty new glazes each week bears evidence of Bacerra's influence.

Any discussion of influence raises the question of imitation. Parallels with Bacerra's work are evident, for example, in the geometric, hard-edge leanings of work by his former students Porntip Sangvanich and Richard McColl (opposite). Before Sangvanich came to the United

**James Haggerty** (United States, b. 1963). From left: *Crater Vase*, 2003. Earthenware. Height: 9 in. (22.9 cm); diameter: 5½ in. (14 cm). *Ruckled Vase*, 2010. Earthenware. Height: 12 in. (30.5 cm); diameter: 4 in. (10.2 cm). *Crater Bowl*, 2014. Earthenware. Height: 5 in. (12.7 cm); diameter: 5½ in. (14 cm). Courtesy of the artist.

States, she studied at the Silpakorn University in Bangkok. Asked about the influence of Bacerra's work, she denied similarities, saying, "Before I came here, I was my own person."[22] Sangvanich's excellent craftsmanship may be her strongest association with Bacerra. McColl cites Frank Stella as his first and deepest influence but credits Bacerra with helping him "refine" his work.[23]

**Porntip Sangvanich** (Thailand, b. 1959), *Points & Counter-points*, 2008. Earthenware. 16½ × 15¼ × 14 in. (41.9 × 38.7 × 35.6 cm). Courtesy of the artist.

**Richard McColl** (United States, b. 1951), *Untitled (Black and White Geometric Construction)*, 1998. Earthenware. 28 × 21 × 7 in. (71.1 × 53.3 × 17.8 cm). Courtesy of the artist.

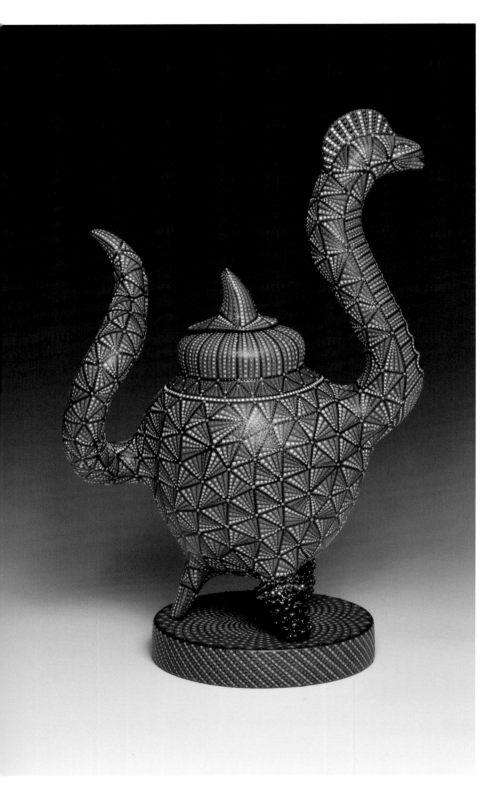

By the 1970s Bacerra began to shift away from reliance on improvisation and spontaneity, toward a more controlled style. His advocacy of what he called "the idea of pure beauty" is illustrated by labor-intensive, nearly obsessive creations that are among the most exquisite and successful examples of visual opulence.[24] He paid no attention to the less-is-more theory or to the idea that compositions require empty space to give the eye a place to rest. He may have viewed the activity in itself as rewarding; maybe he sensed that his investment of time rendered his work more precious.

Describing Bacerra's mature work, Pilcher praised his "unrelenting sense of pattern and color, dependent on having made one good aesthetic decision after another. He was able to integrate the simple act of an accurate gesture, repeated eternally, so that what he did in the last hour had the same sense of directness and freshness as it did in the first hour."[25] Bacerra's former student Ricky Maldonado's persistent dot making bears witness to the same type of compulsive repetition (left).

Summing up his educational theory, Bacerra stated, "It's a philosophy; it's an idea about the material, the technique, about the craftsmanship, about the finish, and the kind of spirit that the piece has that the student will take on and move on and do it in their own way."[26] He stood in opposition to some contemporary art pedagogies and practices. He did not purport to have hidden agendas. His perfectionism implied a partiality for art that showed skill. He felt clay could do anything. In an interview for the Smithsonian Institution Archives of American Art, Frank Lloyd asked Bacerra, "What are the strengths and limitations of the medium of ceramics?" He replied, "I don't know if there are any limitations."[27] Moreover, when it came to clay, Bacerra was a purist.

Above: **Ricky Maldonado** (United States, b. 1953), *Untitled Teapot*, 2011. Earthenware. 18½ × 10 × 7½ in. (47 × 25.4 × 19 cm). Collection of Kelly and Ralph Biase.

Right: **Keiko Fukazawa** (Japan, b. 1955), *Shoot for Tomorrow*, 2001. Ceramic, paint. Diameter: 27 in. (68.6 cm); depth: 3 in. (7.6 cm). Courtesy of the artist.

Keiko Fukazawa, who came from Japan to study at Otis, tells of Bacerra's visit to her studio, where she was experimenting with multimedia works of art. He did not mince words, telling her his negative opinion of mixed media, but, she says, "During the last of his teaching days, Bacerra seemed to have softened his stance."[28] Robert Miller conjectures that "there were two Ralphs": the young, shy, less confident, distant, and uncompromising persona versus the mature, self-possessed, approachable, and more amenable one.[29] Bacerra's personality was likely a mix of both.[30]

As with a teenager who balks at parental authority, sometimes influence creates opposition. Eventually Fukazawa distanced herself from Bacerra's influence and his attitude toward conceptual art. Bacerra stated, "My work is not postmodern in the sense that I am not making any statements—social, political, conceptual, or even intellectual. There is no meaning or metaphor. I am committed more to the idea of pure beauty."[31] Today Fukazawa sees her ideas as important to the artifact. This proclivity can be seen in her plate project, made collaboratively with youth from the California Division of Juvenile Justice (below).

Joan Takayama-Ogawa's work highlights environmental issues, for example, condemning unrestrained consumption of fossil fuels. She also makes realistically detailed works in a trompe l'oeil manner (right) that demonstrate her technical expertise and her assimilation of Bacerra's mantra "know your materials."[32] According to Lois Boardman, an early Chouinard student and friend of Bacerra, "his greatest influence on students was simply knowledge of ceramic materials."[33]

Cindy Kolodziejski, known for her adaptation of the china-painting techniques that she learned from Bacerra, produces conceptual work of a more personal nature. She uses visual language to evoke universal emotions. "I have ideas myself about what the content is, but I

hope to give enough visual information that the viewer will come to the same conclusion."[34] For example, her untitled hourglass form is painted with a female nude lying on her side in a fetal position (opposite, bottom). There is a sense of vulnerability and a sensual or sexual consciousness. A disturbing tension exists between the octopus at one end and the spider pulling at the other extremity.

Perhaps encouraged by Bacerra's latter-day change in his strict clay-only stance, Otis graduates Rich Mudge (left) and Yumi Kiyose have used materials other than clay in their work. Garth Clark and Mark Del Vecchio, whose gallery formerly represented Bacerra, have written on this subject, opening up a new discussion on ceramics. In an essay published on the occasion of the exhibition *One Part Clay*, they write, "The truth is that there is room for both, all-clay and partial-clay are not mutually exclusive. . . . This move to put art ahead of clay signifies a healthy maturity that many of us thought would never arrive."[35]

Whether tangible or intangible, overt or covert, deliberate or accidental, Bacerra's clearest influence came by way of example. His model is the common denominator that unites his students' artistic output. Scott and Naomi Schoenherr, who operate a ceramics studio in Laguna Beach, California, where they create both public art projects and smaller-scale works, note that their teacher's imprint goes beyond methods and techniques, shaping "how we treat the surface of our artworks, as well as how we conduct ourselves as artists."[36]

Opposite, top: **Joan Takayama-Ogawa** (United States, b. 1955), *Made in Pasadena*, 2009. Clay, metal. 7 × 7 × 7 in. (17.8 × 17.8 × 17.8 cm). Courtesy of the artist.

Opposite, bottom: **Cindy Kolodziejski** (Germany, b. 1962), Untitled, 2009. Earthenware, human hair, iron. Length: 24 in. (61 cm); width: 10 in. (25.4 cm). Courtesy of the artist.

Above: **Rich Mudge** (United States, b. 1970), *For 25 Cents # 3 (Barry's Piece)*, 2010. Earthenware, Plexiglas, plastic, electronics. 23 × 13 × 6 in. (58.4 × 33 × 15.2 cm). Courtesy of the artist.

## NOTES

1. Chouinard Art Institute was founded in 1921. In 1961 California Institute of the Arts was established through the merger of Chouinard and the Los Angeles Conservatory of Music. Otis was founded in 1918 as the Otis Art Institute of the Los Angeles Museum of History, Science and Art. The school went through various name changes, becoming Otis College of Art and Design in 1993.

2. *Crossroads in Clay at Chouinard and Otis: The Ralph Bacerra Years* will be on view at the Vincent Price Art Museum at East Los Angeles College, Monterey Park, California, from September 19 to December 5, 2015.

3. Ralph Bacerra, in *Art Is What I Do: The Life of Ralph Bacerra*, directed by Jo Lauria and produced by the Boardman Family Foundation in cooperation with Otis College of Art and Design (2008), Vimeo video, 25:50, posted by Otis College of Art and Design, 2014, https://vimeo.com/90053300.

4. Ralph Bacerra, oral history interview conducted by Frank Lloyd, April 7–19, 2004, Archives of American Art, Smithsonian Institution.

5. Suki Diamond, telephone interview with the author, April 12, 2015.

6. Don Pilcher, telephone interview with the author, April 20, 2015.

7. International Pipe and Ceramics (Interpace)—a Los Angeles–based ceramics firm known as Gladding, McBean prior to 1962—donated colored underglazes, china paint, and lusters to Chouinard.

8. Sharon Jeniye, interview with the author, March 7, 2015.

9. Works by a number of Bacerra's international students are included in the *Crossroads in Clay* exhibition: Tetsuji Aono, Keiko Fukazawa, Jun Kaneko, Yumi Kiyose, Mineo Mizuno, and Porntip Sangvanich.

10. Lin Werner, telephone interview with the author, April 15, 2015.

11. Suki Diamond, telephone interview with the author, April 12, 2015.

12. Leonard Skuro, telephone interview with the author, May 2, 2015.

13. Ibid.

14. Juanita Jimenez, telephone interview with the author, April 27, 2015.

15. Bonnie Ikemura, telephone interview with the author, April 20, 2015.

16. *California Design Ten* (Pasadena, CA: Pasadena Art Museum, 1968), 104; *California Design Eleven* (Pasadena, CA: Pasadena Art Museum, 1971), 124.

17. Adrian Saxe, in *Art Is What I Do*.

18. Peter Shire, oral history interview conducted by Jo Lauria, September 18–19, 2007, Archives of American Art, Smithsonian Institution.

19. This texture glaze, formulated by Otto Heino, was called "Otto's texture" by Bacerra's students.

20. The exhibition featured new work by alumni who attended Otis's Graduate Fine Arts program between 1989 and 2009.

21. James Haggerty, telephone interview with the author, May 1, 2015. Haggerty's enrollment is confirmed by roll books for Bacerra's classes; courtesy of Porntip Sangvanich. See also Linda Janos, "Luminosity: James Haggerty's Low-Fire Lusters," *Ceramics Monthly* 53 (November 2005): 57.

22. Porntip Sangvanich, telephone interview with the author, April 10, 2015.

23. Richard McColl, telephone interview with the author, April 15, 2015.

24. Ralph Bacerra, in Jo Lauria, "Ralph Bacerra—Ceramic Artist," *Ceramics: Art and Perception*, no. 15 (1994): 18.

25. Don Pilcher, telephone interview with the author, April 20, 2015.

26. Ralph Bacerra, in *Art Is What I Do*.

27. Ralph Bacerra, oral history interview conducted by Frank Lloyd, April 7–19, 2004, Archives of American Art, Smithsonian Institution.

28. Keiko Fukazawa, telephone interview with the author, April 13, 2015.

29. Robert Miller, interview with the author, February 3, 2015.

30. Don Pilcher, telephone interview with the author, April 20, 2015.

31. Bacerra, in Lauria, "Ralph Bacerra," 18.

32. Joan Takayama-Ogawa, interview with the author, April 27, 2015.

33. Lois Boardman, telephone interview with the author, May 4, 2015.

34. Cindy Kolodziejski, telephone interview with the author, May 1, 2015.

35. Garth Clark and Mark Del Vecchio, "One Part Clay," in *One Part Clay: Ceramic Avant-garde and Mixed Media* (New York: Dean Project, 2006), 24.

36. Scott and Naomi Schoenherr, quoted in Katey Schultz, "Studio Visit: Scott and Naomi Schoenherr," *Ceramics Monthly* 61 (October 2013): 31.

## FURTHER READING

**Clark, Garth.** *A Century of Ceramics in the United States, 1878–1978: A Study of Its Development.* New York: Dutton; Syracuse, NY: Everson Museum of Art, 1979.

———, ed. *Ceramic Millennium: Critical Writings on Ceramic History, Theory, and Art.* Halifax: Press of the Nova Scotia College of Art and Design, 2006.

**Johnson, Christy, Martha Longenecker-Roth, and Marguerite McIntosh.** *Harrison McIntosh: A Timeless Legacy.* Pomona, CA: American Museum of Ceramic Art, 2009.

**Lauria, Jo.** *Color and Fire: Defining Moments in Studio Ceramics, 1950–2000.* Los Angeles: Los Angeles County Museum of Art, 2000.

**Lauria, Jo, and Suzanne Baizerman.** *California Design: The Legacy of West Coast Craft and Style.* San Francisco: Chronicle, 2005.

**Levin, Elaine.** *The History of American Ceramics, 1607 to the Present: From Pipkins and Bean Pots to Contemporary Forms.* New York: Abrams, 1988.

———, ed. *Movers and Shakers in American Ceramics: Defining Twentieth-Century Ceramics; A Collection of Articles from "Ceramics Monthly."* Westerville, OH: American Ceramic Society, 2003.

# vincent price
## ART MUSEUM

**Participants in *Crossroads in Clay at Chouinard and Otis: The Ralph Bacerra Years:***

### CHOUNARD STUDENTS

Harry Berman

Sharon Jeniye-Cohen

Suki Diamond

Bonnie Ikemura

Juanita Jimenez

Jun Kaneko

Mineo Mizuno

Don Pilcher

Elsa Rady

Adrian Saxe

Peter Shire

Leonard Skuro

Lin Werner

### OTIS STUDENTS

Tetsuji Aono

Keiko Fukazawa

James Haggerty

Marc Hoar

Stanton Hunter

Yumi Kiyose

Kathleen Klein-Wakefield

Jean Kojima

Cindy Kolodziejski

Ricky Maldonado

Richard McColl

Robert Miller

Rich Mudge

Kevin Myers

Diego Romero

Porntip Sangvanich

Scott Schoenherr

Joan Takayama-Ogawa

**Ralph Bacerra**, *Untitled Sculpture*, 1972. Ceramic. 39½ × 16 × 12 in. (100.3 × 40.6 × 30.5 cm). Collection of George and Connie Bacerra.

Left: **Ralph Bacerra**, *Untitled Female Figure/Tang*, 1994. Whiteware. 29 × 10 × 7 in. (73.7 × 25.4 × 17.8 cm). Collection of Patti and Mike Marcus.

Above: **Ralph Bacerra**, *Untitled Teapot*, 2005. Ceramic. 20½ × 14 × 5½ in. (52.1 × 35.6 × 14 cm). Collection of Mary Coquillard.

Overleaf: Customers lining up to gain entrance to the ceramics sale at Chouinard Art Institute (left) and waiting to pay for their purchases (right), 1960.

# Chronology

JO LAURIA AND MACKENZIE FARGO

1

2, 3

4

## 1938

Ralph Bacerra is born in Garden Grove, California, to Candido Bacerra and Audrey Williamson. Candido, who was from the Philippines, immigrated to the United States in the 1930s. While employed as a farmworker in Montana, he met Audrey—a young woman of English descent—and they were married. The Bacerras moved to California in the late 1930s and settled in the Orange County community of Garden Grove in a house that bordered agricultural farmland. This is where they raised their five children—Joann, Ralph, Frederick, George, and Philip—and the children worked on the nearby farm packaging fruits and vegetables to be trucked to market. Candido and Audrey would eventually divorce.

FIG. 1.  The Bacerras' five children in front of their house on Sugar Street, Garden Grove, c. 1950: (back row, from left) Joann and Ralph, (middle row) Frederick and George, and (in front) Philip.

FIG. 2.  Candido (kneeling) and sons George (left) and Ralph in front of their Toddy Street House, Santa Ana, c. 1960.

FIG. 3.  Audrey standing between her sons Philip (left) and Ralph, c. 1962.

## 1955

Bacerra graduates from Garden Grove High School. Following graduation, he enrolls at Orange Coast Junior College, Costa Mesa (now Orange Coast College).

FIG. 4.  Ralph Bacerra at the time of his high school graduation, 1955.

I went to Orange Coast Junior College, where I became involved with the art department there and I took a ceramics class, and I said, "Well, this is sort of fun." And after two years I decided to go to an art school and decided upon Chouinard over Otis or Art Center because they had a ceramic department. Entered an art school, and as an elective I took a ceramic course and decided this is where I want to be and I stayed. So that's some forty years ago.

—RALPH BACERRA[1]

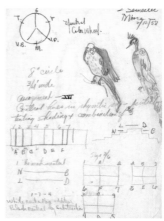

9

5, 6

7, 8

## 1957–58

Bacerra enrolls at Chouinard Art Institute with the intention of majoring in advertising and commercial art. As part of the curricular requirements for the major, he takes William Moore's yearlong Introductory Design class in the 1957–58 academic year. From Moore, Bacerra learns the core principles of design and color theory and, most importantly, benefits from his legendary "methods of framing and assigning a problem" and his emphasis on student critiques as a teaching tool.

FIGS. 5, 6. Pages from Bacerra's notebook/sketchbook from his Introductory Design class at Chouinard with instructor William Moore, 1957–58. These pages illustrate an assignment for working through concepts of composition, color relationships, and shading—as demonstrated by Bacerra's sketches of fluttering insects.

Bacerra enrolls in Vivika Heino's ceramics class as an elective during his first year at Chouinard. Thus begins his love affair with clay. Determined to work in this medium, he switches his major from advertising and commercial art to ceramics.

Heino was a benevolent taskmaster regarding knowledge of materials and techniques. She taught students the fundamental skills they would need to function as independent studio potters: clay composition; forming methods such as wheel throwing, coiling, and slab construction; mold making and slip casting; glaze calculation; kiln building and operation; and basic business principles. Her husband, Otto Heino, also participated as a "team teacher," although he was not formally a faculty member. Bacerra formed a lifelong relationship with the Heinos and considered them his mentors and close friends.

Vivika Heino recognized Bacerra's talent for working with clay and advocated for him to receive scholarships. Eventually she appointed him as the studio "tech," which enabled him to receive a tuition waiver.

FIG. 7. Ralph Bacerra and Vivika Heino at Chouinard Art Institute, Los Angeles, 1958. Ralph Bacerra papers, Archives of American Art, Smithsonian Institution.

FIG. 8. Vivika and Otto Heino working in the ceramics studio at Chouinard Art Institute, Los Angeles, 1958.

FIG. 9. Bacerra compiled a small spiral-bound notebook in which he showcased his two Awards of Merit won at the student competition in ceramics in 1958—one for second place, one for honorable mention—and examples of his finished ceramics.

10

12

11

13

## 1960

As part of their training, ceramics students at Chouinard acquire the skills to produce, display, and sell their pottery during the school's ceramics sale. These annual events are eagerly anticipated in the Los Angeles art community, and buyers line up to get in.

FIG. 10. Customers lining up at the Chouinard Art Institute ceramics sale, 1960.

## 1961

Bacerra shows early promise as a potter, proving his mettle at the wheel. He learns how to throw pots quickly, efficiently, and prolifically, much the way a production potter functions. One of his former students at Chouinard, the artist Peter Shire, recalled watching Bacerra throw pots on the wheel, describing him as having "butterfly hands."[2]

FIG. 11. Cups, bottles, and vases that Bacerra created on the potter's wheel and placed outside on bats to dry, c. 1960.

Bacerra graduates from Chouinard Art Institute with a BFA.

FIG. 12. An inside spread from Bacerra's bound portfolio of photographs of his ceramic works created in 1960–61. It is likely that he had to produce this portfolio as part of the graduation requirements for the ceramics major.

FIG. 13. Two pages from Bacerra's portfolio, featuring a thrown covered jar and a slab-constructed sculptural vessel form, 1960–61. It is revealing that from the very beginning of his career he made both functional and sculptural pieces.

## 1961–63

To avoid the draft, Bacerra enlists in the army and serves for two years. Although he joined the army "to see the world," to his disappointment, he is stationed at Fort MacArthur in San Pedro, about twenty-five miles from downtown Los Angeles. This turns out to be advantageous as he and Vivika Heino are able to keep in contact. On his discharge in 1963, Heino asks him to teach a pottery class in the summer session. This teaching experience proves invaluable: when the Heinos leave Chouinard before the fall semester of that year—Vivika had been offered a teaching position at Rhode Island School of Design—Bacerra takes over their responsibilities at the school's ceramics studio. For the year following the Heinos' departure, Bacerra shares teaching responsibilities for the ceramics department with John Fassbinder.

14 15 16 17

## 1963

Bacerra enrolls in a three-week workshop at the University of Southern California (USC) to watch the esteemed Japanese potter Shōji Hamada work at the wheel and glaze his pieces. At the end of the workshop, Hamada spoke about each pot individually—espousing his philosophy about the essence or spirit of the pot—with his son translating. In his oral history interview for the Archives of American Art, Bacerra recalled, "It was a great experience. There were about 20 people and [Hamada]—you watched him come in and work. He came in with his kimonos, and he sat cross-legged on his table and used a stick to turn his wheel, but it all worked for him, and he worked very quietly."[3]

Susan Peterson, head of the ceramics department at USC at the time and a great admirer of Hamada, had invited the Japanese master potter to conduct the workshop. (Peterson would publish a monograph on Hamada in 1974.)

FIG. 14 Bacerra in his full-dress army uniform, c. 1961–63.

FIG. 15 Bacerra watching Shōji Hamada apply the finishing details to a teapot during a workshop demonstration, ceramics studio, University of Southern California, 1963.

## 1964

Bacerra is appointed chairman of the Chouinard ceramics department, which is an extraordinary achievement and responsibility for a twenty-six-year-old. During this time he purchases a house in Eagle Rock and establishes his first studio on his property there.

FIG. 16 Ralph Bacerra, c. 1964.

## 1967

Ken Deavers founds the American Hand gallery in the Georgetown area of Washington, DC, devoting the modest space to showing ceramics. Deavers starts out showing principally California ceramists, as he grew up in California and feels a kinship with artists from his home state. (Eventually the American Hand would expand its roster to include artists beyond California and show glass, fiber, and prints as well as ceramics.)

Deavers discovers Bacerra's small, graceful ceramic bottle forms at the Canyon Gallery in Topanga, California, and is impressed by their elegant lines (fig. 17). He begins showing Bacerra's work at American Hand in 1967 and continues to do so until 1997. The gallery officially closes in 2000.

FIG. 17 Ralph Bacerra, *Untitled Bottle*, c. 1968. Glazed porcelain. Height: 7 in. (17.8 cm); diameter: 4 in. (10.2 cm). Collection of Lois and Robert Boardman.

18                                    19                                    20, 21

## 1968

As a teacher Bacerra follows the structured paradigm established at Chouinard by Vivika Heino. He develops the students' skill set by teaching a rigorous program emphasizing clay and glaze composition and the full spectrum of clay-forming techniques. "Know your materials" is one of his mantras for success in the studio.

As head of the ceramics department, Bacerra oversees the planning and execution of the annual ceramics sale, as Heino did before him. The earnings from these sales fund scholarships and the purchase of materials and equipment. During the fall semester students produce work for the sale, and all participate in the setup and display of the merchandise as well as working on the day of the sale. A receipt dated December 9, 1967, indicates that the proceeds from the annual sale totaled $7,437.63, the equivalent of more than $50,000 in 2015.[4]

**FIG. 18**  Bacerra (seated) with his students (from left) Peter Shire, George Gee, Juanita Jimenez, and Mineo Mizuno in the ceramics studio, Chouinard Art Institute, 1968.

**FIG. 19**  Poster announcing the 15th Annual Ceramics Sale at California Institute of the Arts / Chouinard, 1968. Featured are (back row, from left) Bacerra, Peter Shire, and Adrian Saxe; the woman in the center is Nancy Chunn, and to her right is Juanita Jimenez. The names of the other two women are unknown. According to Peter Shire, Bacerra and Shire are holding "huge pots" that Bacerra and Jimenez threw, "being they were the only ones that could handle so much clay." Additionally, Shire recollects: "Adrian [Saxe] dreamed up the concept of the black and white format to capitalize on the high resolution/high contrast look that was so important at that moment."[5]

**FIG. 20**  Bacerra giving student Lin Werner an impromptu critique, Chouinard ceramics studio, 1970.

**FIG. 21**  Three of Bacerra's large-scale glazed stoneware sculptures were juried into the exhibition California Design Ten, Pasadena Art Museum, 1968.

From left: *Red, Brown, Metallic Form*; height: 24 in. (61 cm), diameter: 18 in. (45.7 cm). *Black and Red Form*, height: 37 in. (94 cm); diameter: 12 in. (30.5 cm). *Green, Orange, Black and White Form*, height: 36 in. (91.4 cm); diameter: 11 in. (28 cm).

## 1969

Bacerra's work *Orange Form* (1968; p. 17) is included in the groundbreaking touring exhibition *Objects: USA*, curated by Lee Nordness, and is documented in the accompanying book.

22

23, 24

FASAR... THE COOKING METHOD THAT OBSOLETES ALL OTHERS

25

## 1970

Since 1962 Chouinard had been in the process of merging with California Institute of the Arts (CalArts). By 1970 the faculty and students are aware that the Los Angeles Grand View campus would be closed and that Chouinard Art Institute would no longer exist as an independent college. It would be absorbed into CalArts when the school moved to its completed Valencia campus in 1972. This is particularly devastating for the ceramics department as CalArts administrators had decided to eliminate ceramics from the curriculum. Bacerra and his students are acutely aware that classes in the spring semester of 1971 would be the last taught in the Chouinard ceramics studio. As a visual lament, they enact a mock funeral, and a photograph of the event appears on the poster announcing the 17th Annual Ceramic Sale, with the abbreviation R.I.P. as the last line of the announcement (fig. 22).

FIG. 22  Poster announcing the 17th Annual Ceramic Sale, the final sale before the closing of Chouinard, 1970. Dressed in black and wearing a bowler hat, Bacerra helps carry a wooden coffin as part of a funeral procession staged to protest the "death" of ceramics at Chouinard.

FIG. 23  Three of Bacerra's impressively scaled glazed earthenware sculptures were displayed in the juried exhibition California Design Eleven, Pasadena Art Museum, 1971. From left: *Candado*, height: 60 in. (152.4 cm); *Ibo*, height: 60 in. (152.4 cm); and *Caribe*, height: 54 in. (137.2 cm).

## 1971

Ron Cunningham, Bacerra's partner, pioneers an electromagnetic induction heating system for ceramic cooktops that he markets under the name Fasar. Bacerra develops the clay and glaze composition and creates original designs for the ceramic tiles that are used in the cooktops. From 1971 through 1975 he personally glazes the tiles for Fasar ranges. Thereafter, ceramic decal patterns that Bacerra designed are applied to the tiles by different production facilities, and custom tile orders are executed by Lin Werner and Porntip Sangvanich, both former Bacerra students (at Chouinard and Otis, respectively). Fasar would go out of business in the 1980s, but the induction heating stovetop was distributed and sold under other company names until 1995.[6]

FIG. 24  Fasar company brochure touting ceramic cooktops as the latest innovation in cooking, c. 1975. The ceramic tiles shown in this promotional photograph were decorated with decal patterns designed by Bacerra.

FIG. 25  A decal produced from a design that Bacerra created for Fasar cooktop tiles. Having decals made of his various designs liberated him from the labor of handcrafting unique tiles and provided Fasar with an inventory of tile patterns to offer customers.

26

27

## 1972

Bacerra's standing as an internationally recognized artist is confirmed when his work is included in the exhibition International Ceramics 1972 at the Victoria and Albert Museum, London, and the National Museum of Modern Art, Kyoto, and documented in the accompanying catalog.

## 1975

With Ron Cunningham, Bacerra purchases a grander, more spacious home with a pool on Patrician Way, Pasadena. Bacerra builds a large studio on the property and a one-thousand-square-foot greenhouse, where he grows exotic flowers, most notably orchids.

FIG. 26　Bacerra on the deck surrounding his house in Pasadena. Displayed behind him is one of his untitled animal forms (1980s).

## 1976

Bacerra is invited to have a one-person show at Theo Portnoy Gallery, New York. His first show features the sculptural animal forms, and subsequent solo shows in 1980 and 1983 focus on large porcelain platters and lidded vessels decorated with overglaze painting.

FIG. 27　Bacerra at Theo Portnoy Gallery during his solo show, 1980.

FIG. 28　Ralph Bacerra, *Covered Container*, 1979–80. Porcelain, glaze, and overglaze enamel painting. 9 × 15 × 15 in. (22.9 × 38.1 × 38.1 cm).

Pieces from this series were included in Bacerra's solo exhibition at Theo Portnoy Gallery, New York, 1980.

28

## 1977

Bacerra is the invited artist for the 1977 Making It in Clay workshop, held at Montgomery College in Maryland. The workshops were cosponsored by Eagle Ceramics and the American Hand gallery in cooperation with the college. The guest artist had to commit to a three-day program: Friday night lecture and slide presentation, Saturday workshop demonstration, and Sunday opening of an exhibition of the artist's work at the American Hand. This invitation provided Bacerra with the opportunity to have his first solo show at the gallery. For the exhibition he created large porcelain platters and lidded stacked boxes decorated with glazes, overglaze enamels, and metallic lusters, presenting a total of thirty-one pieces.

*Those thirty-one pieces sold in fifteen minutes; people were so crazy to get his work they were lined up outside the gallery starting at nine o'clock in the morning. We didn't open until one in the afternoon, and people came rushing through the door. It got so crazy we just said, "Go stand by your piece otherwise you're going to lose it." And it was all gone in fifteen minutes. Ralph was there, and he was just astonished by the reaction to his work.*

—KEN DEAVERS,
FOUNDER OF THE AMERICAN HAND GALLERY[7]

FIG. 29 Ralph Bacerra, *Stacking Porcelain Bowls*, c. 1977. Porcelain. Height: 7¼ in. (18.4 cm); diameter: 6¾ in. (17.1 cm). American Museum of Ceramic Art, Gift of James W. and Jackie Voell, 2005.2.0031.

29

## 1980

The decade from 1980 to 1990 is a very productive and inspired period for Bacerra. During these years his career—both as a professional artist and as a teacher—blossoms.

In 1980 Bacerra embarked on the first of several trips to Asia, visiting Japan, Korea, Taiwan, and Hong Kong. He revisited these countries on subsequent trips and also traveled to Singapore and the Philippines. His travel companions included Cunningham as well as Lin Werner and Lois Boardman, former Chouinard students who were now friends. The objective of their travels was to learn about Asian art and experience the culture.

They visited museums, gardens, and historical landmarks and sought out sites related to pottery whenever possible. In Japan, Bacerra was intrigued and impressed by the overglaze enamel painting on Imari, Kutani, and Nabeshima wares and searched for shops where he could purchase the overglaze enamel pigments and fine brushes used to execute the delicate designs. In Taiwan he was enthralled by the imperial collection of Chinese ceramics on display at the National Palace Museum, especially the variations of celadon glazes and the exquisite blue-and-white porcelains dating from the fourteenth to the eighteenth century.

On his return from Asia, Bacerra resolutely determined to master the techniques of overglaze enamel painting (also referred to as "china painting") and underglaze painting with cobalt oxide, as expertly practiced by Persian and Chinese potters of centuries past. He began collecting excellent examples of Asian pottery to closely study shapes, glazes, color combinations, and design schemes.

**FIG. 30** Ralph Bacerra, *Test Plate for Overglaze Enamels*, early 1980s. Porcelain. Height: 1 in. (2.5 cm); diameter: 12 in. (30.5 cm).

Bacerra made this porcelain plate to test the colors of overglaze enamel pigments and to determine the correct saturation of cobalt oxide for use in blue-and-white underglaze painting. To identify each color after firing the plate in the kiln, he recorded the number of the overglaze pigment alongside his brushstrokes.

**FIG. 31** Ralph Bacerra, *Untitled Dinner Plate*, c. early 1980s. Ceramic. Height: 1 in. (2.5 cm); diameter: 12 in. (30.5 cm).

This plate, part of a dinnerware set that Bacerra created in the early 1980s, is one of the artist's first successful series to showcase his newly acquired skill in applying overglaze enamels.

**FIG. 32** Ralph Bacerra, *Untitled Platter*, c. 1980s. Ceramic. 3 × 16 × 11 in. (7.6 × 40.6 × 27.9 cm).

This platter is an excellent example of Bacerra's early development of the underglaze blue-and-white and overglaze enamel painting techniques.

33

34

## 1980 (CONTINUED)

In addition to Asian travels, classes in Ikebana flower arranging, combined with the intense scrutiny of the iris through participation in the Iris Society, broaden Bacerra's understanding of shape and pattern.[8] He translates these experiences into making basket forms for Ikebana containers and holistically integrates the iris motif into his design vocabulary.

> FIG. 33  Bacerra participated in an ikebana flower-arranging class taught by "sensei" Mrs. Kodoma. The class was held at Lin Werner's Santa Monica studio in the early 1980s.

> FIG. 34  Ralph Bacerra, *Untitled Platter with Handle*, c. 1980s. Stoneware. 1½ × 12½ × 7½ in. (3.8 × 31.8 × 19.1 cm). Collection of Porntip Sangvanich.

> FIG. 35  Ralph Bacerra, *Untitled Platter*, c. 1980. Porcelain with overglaze enamel painting and metallic lusters. Height: 3 in. (7.6 cm); diameter: 22¾ in. (57.8 cm). Private collection.

## 1981

The Garth Clark Gallery opens in Los Angeles, and Bacerra is one of the original twelve artists invited to be part of its roster. By 1983 Clark opens a gallery in New York City. The gallery has representation in Kansas City and London for periods of time, but the New York gallery becomes the primary space after the L.A. gallery closes in the mid-1990s. Bacerra's work is shown at all gallery locations and is featured almost every year in solo exhibitions in Los Angeles or New York until the Garth Clark Gallery formally closes in 2006.

*Ralph's constancy was one of his great qualities. He was loyal and had a sense of quality and commitment to those standards that never wavered.*

—GARTH CLARK AND MARK DEL VECCHIO[9]

## 1982

After an eleven-year hiatus, Bacerra returns to the classroom, accepting an invitation to teach ceramics part-time at what is then known as Otis Art Institute of Parsons School of Design. The first two classes that he teaches are Surface Design and Glaze Calculation.

36

37

## 1983

Bacerra is appointed chair of the ceramics department at Otis. He holds this position until Otis closes its campus near MacArthur Park in 1996.

> FIG. 36  Bacerra's faculty ID card issued by Otis Art Institute of Parsons School of Design. (Otis and Parsons were affiliated between 1978 and 1993.)

## 1984

Bacerra's work is included in the exhibition *Art in Clay: 1950's to 1980's in Southern California; Evolution, Revolution, Continuation* and reproduced in the accompanying catalog. The Los Angeles Municipal Art Gallery hosts the exhibition (July 24–August 26, 1984) as part of the city's Olympic Arts Festival.

## 1987

Garth Clark's *American Ceramics, 1876 to the Present* is published. Illustrations of Bacerra's *Orange Form* (1968), *Soup Tureen* (1978), and *Untitled Platter* (1986) are included. Describing the artist's work, Clark writes: "Bacerra's plates now are host to an equally complex, illusory painting of floating boxes, cylinders, and triangles—moving from the surface into the conceptual volumes of 'potter's space.'"[10]

> FIG. 37  Bacerra in his Eagle Rock studio with platters in various states of completion. He was making work for his one-person exhibition at Garth Clark Gallery, 1986. It was characteristic of him to work on many pieces at the same time, and because of the possibility of breakage, he typically made three times the number of works he intended to include in any given exhibition.

> FIG. 38  Ralph Bacerra, *Untitled Platter,* 1986. Earthenware with underglaze, glaze, and overglaze painting. Height: 3 ⅜ in. (8.6 cm); diameter: 23 in. (58.4 cm). Collection of Garth Clark and Mark Del Vecchio.

> This is one of the series of large platters that Bacerra made for a solo exhibition at Garth Clark Gallery in 1986, and it is still a personal favorite of Garth Clark and Mark Del Vecchio.

39

40

41, 42

43

## 1988

Elaine Levin publishes *The History of American Ceramics, 1607 to the Present: From Pipkins and Bean Pots to Contemporary Forms*, which features an illustration of Bacerra's glazed porcelain *Wall Piece* (1983). Levin writes of Bacerra, "By 1979 his dominant image was that of birds in flight. Interlocking geometric and organic shapes (reminiscent of a technique used by M. C. Escher) now directed Bacerra's concerns where birds and patterns meld in an overload of visual information." [11]

> FIG. 39 Ralph Bacerra, *Untitled Platter*, 1984. Ceramic. 3 × 25 × 18 in. (7.6 × 63.5 × 45.7 cm). Collection of Alan Mandell.
>
> This piece is from the same series as the one illustrated in Elaine Levin's book.

## 1989–90

Bacerra brings to Otis the same central teaching principles that he had established at Chouinard. (See Christy Johnson's essay in this volume.) His approach is hands-on, and he frequently works alongside the students in the studio, practicing, as Peter Voulkos had before him, the art of teaching through working.

> FIG. 40 Bacerra working at the potter's wheel on a vessel, Otis ceramics studio, c. 1989–90.
>
> FIG. 41 Otis ceramics studio, c. 1989–90. Frequently Bacerra helped students with challenging studio projects. With his guidance, student Robert Miller created this gigantic wheel-thrown and coiled vessel.
>
> FIG. 42 Bacerra hosted a wedding reception at his home in Pasadena for his niece Cindy Lee Bass, 1990. Bacerra's brother Frederick (left) attended the reception.
>
> FIG. 43 Bacerra with the legendary Dada and ceramic artist Beatrice Wood, c. 1990.

Bacerra makes the pilgrimage to Ojai, California, to visit Beatrice Wood at her home and studio. Wood was very fond of Bacerra and promised to give him her secret formulas for luster glazes on the condition that he would not use them on his ceramics until she died. He was given the formulas and, in turn, honored Wood's request.

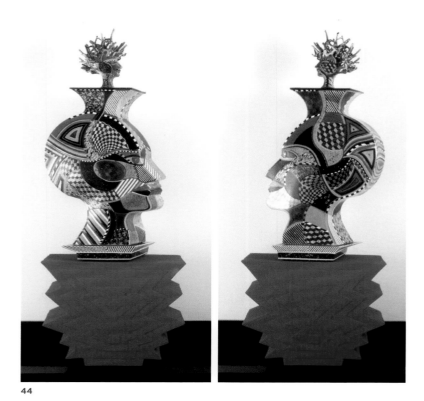

44

45

## 1990

*Clay Today: Contemporary Ceramists and Their Work; A Catalogue of the Howard and Gwen Laurie Smits Collection at the Los Angeles County Museum of Art*, written by Martha Drexler Lynn, is published by the Los Angeles County Museum of Art and Chronicle Books. The book includes an extended biography of Bacerra and an illustration of a large porcelain bowl with overglaze enamel painting of interlocking birds—now recognized as one of his signature motifs.

## 1991

Bacerra completes a private commission for an installation of two majestic portrait vessels, each mounted on a tall flame-red base (fig. 44). This commission reaffirmed his mastery of large, complex forms and his ability to execute critically significant commissioned works on time and to a client's specifications. The works were installed in the dining area of a private home.

FIG. 44  Ralph Bacerra, *Pair of Portrait Vessels*, 1991. Whiteware. 54 × 22 × 10 in. (137.2 × 55.9 × 25.4 cm) overall. Private collection.

## 1992

Bacerra is invited to participate in the International Invitational Exhibition of Contemporary Ceramic Art, National Museum of History, Taipei, Taiwan. His *Untitled Portrait Vessel* (1991) and *Untitled Teapot* (1989) are both selected for the exhibition.

## 1996

Founded by Frank Lloyd, the Frank Lloyd Gallery, Modern and Contemporary Ceramic Art, officially opens in January in the Bergamot Station arts complex, Santa Monica. The gallery represents Bacerra continuously from its inception until it closes in February 2015.

*I chose Ralph Bacerra because his work was technically brilliant, and he was an established artist. . . . Ralph was reliable and timely, disciplined and responsible. He was able to produce complex work, meet deadlines, and was willing to do commissions—in short, an art dealer's dream.—Frank Lloyd* [12]

FIG. 45  Artists represented by Frank Lloyd Gallery, 2001. The artists posed outside the gallery during John Mason's major one-person show there. Front row, from left: Peter Shire, Anna Silver, John Mason, Phil Cornelius, Roseline Delisle, and Cindy Kolodziejski. Back row, from left: Richard Shaw, Robert Hudson, Ralph Bacerra, Tony Marsh, and Frank Lloyd.

46

47, 48

Otis College closes its central Los Angeles campus and relocates to a new facility in the city's Westchester neighborhood. As part of the relocation strategy, and in an effort to reduce costs, the discipline of ceramics is eliminated from the fine arts curriculum. At this juncture, Bacerra decides to retire from teaching. His longtime friends and supporters Lois and Bob Boardman plan a surprise retirement party for him at their home. Bacerra is indeed surprised by the more than two hundred friends and former students who attend the celebration.

**FIG. 46** Bacerra happily wore the celebratory horseshoe-shaped wreath (the kind given to winning horses) presented to him at the surprise retirement party in his honor, May 1996.

## 1997

Although Bacerra is noted for his rounded, volumetric forms, he produces a series of "pillow boxes" with domed covers (fig. 47). The boxes, similar to his round covered vessels made on the potter's wheel, are actually treated like two-part vessels but are made by the slab construction method. As such, they are hollow forms that contain interior space and also provide a contiguous clay canvas on which to apply his design scheme.

**FIG. 47** Ralph Bacerra, *Covered Vessel*, 1997. Ceramic. 7½ × 21 × 17 in. (19.1 × 53.3 × 43.2 cm). Collection of Paul and Sharon Dauer.

**FIG. 48** Bacerra's large *Untitled Lidded Vessel* in situ at Empress Court Restaurant, Caesars Palace, Las Vegas. Bacerra received the commission from Neal Menzies & Company, Beverly Hills.

## 1998

Bacerra is acknowledged as an honorary member of the National Conference on Education for the Ceramic Arts at the annual conference in Fort Worth, Texas, in "recognition of outstanding accomplishment and notable contributions to the ceramic arts." He had repeatedly commented to friends and colleagues that teaching was an equal exchange and that he received "as much from the students as he gave." He was a dedicated and passionate educator, and many of his students became lifelong friends and supporters. A tradition of annual luncheons in L.A.'s Chinatown to celebrate Bacerra's birthday on January 23 began after his retirement from Otis and continued through the year of his death.

49

50

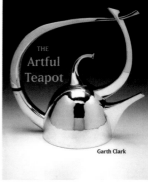

51

52

## 1999

Garth Clark Gallery, New York, organizes *Ralph Bacerra: A Survey* and publishes an accompanying catalog. Selected works from Bacerra's signature series of teapots, chargers, portrait vessels, cloud vessels, and large lidded vessels are shown, representing, according to gallery owners Garth Clark and Mark Del Vecchio, the "highest points" of Bacerra's career.[13]

Bacerra is named a fellow of the American Craft Council for demonstrated "leadership in the field, outstanding ability as an artist and/ or teacher, and 25 years or more of professional achievement as an American craftsperson."

## 2000

Bacerra's ceramics are featured in the exhibition *Color and Fire: Defining Moments in Studio Ceramics, 1950–2000* at the Los Angeles County Museum of Art, and several of his pieces—sculptural vessels and an animal form—are reproduced in the exhibition catalog. Further, the film produced in conjunction with the exhibition includes an interview with Bacerra, in one of the rare times that he was captured speaking on film.[14]

FIG. 49 Opening of the exhibition *Color and Fire* at the Los Angeles County Museum of Art, 2000. Mark Del Vecchio and Ralph Bacerra stand in the galleries with Bacerra's *Untitled Animal Form* (1976). Both men are holding copies of the accompanying catalog.

FIG. 50 The brothers Bacerra pose for a photograph after a memorial service for their youngest brother, Philip—George on the left, Ralph in the middle, and Frederick on the right—in 2000. The reception after the memorial took place at the Orange County home of George and Connie Bacerra.

## 2001

Garth Clark's book *The Artful Teapot*—which features illustrations of two of Bacerra's teapots, *Teapot (branch)* (1989) and *Cloud Vessel* (1997)—is published.[15]

FIG. 51 Cover of *The Artful Teapot* by Garth Clark.

FIG. 52 Bacerra standing between two of his untitled lidded vessels in his Eagle Rock studio, 2001. He completed these works in preparation for a solo exhibition that year at Garth Clark Gallery, New York.

Bacerra is commissioned to make four monumental covered vessels for the restaurant at the Four Seasons Hotel in San Francisco. Covered with a metallic gold glaze, the vessels are placed in various locations in the dining room and become focal points of the vistas.

FIG. 53 Ralph Bacerra, *Untitled Gold Vessel*, 2001. Earthenware. Height: 31½ in. (80 cm); diameter: 22 in. (55.9 cm).

This vessel is from the same series as those Bacerra made for the restaurant at the Four Seasons Hotel, San Francisco. The overall lustrous gold glaze makes this large-scale vessel spectacularly opulent.

**Ralph Bacerra**
**1938–2008**

54                                          55                                          56

FIG. 54  From left: Bacerra, Peter Shire, and Adrian Saxe at an opening at Frank Lloyd Gallery, Bergamot Station, 2002. Shire and Saxe were students of Bacerra's at Chouinard in the late 1960s and early 1970s.

## 2003

As part of the City of Pasadena Public Art Program, Bacerra is commissioned by Maguire Partners to create a tile mural for the east wall of Western Asset Plaza, 385 Colorado Boulevard, Pasadena. Titled *Kaloseidos (Beauty and Form)*, the mural is composed of more than three thousand tiles—designed, handmade, and glazed by Bacerra. The artist also oversees the installation and completion of the mural on-site.

FIG. 55  Ralph Bacerra, *Tile Sample for Western Asset Commission: Study for Mural*, 2003. Ceramic, wood frame. 29¾ × 23½ × 1¼ in. (73.7 × 59.7 × 3.2 cm) framed. Collection of Porntip Sangvanich.

Glazed tile sample for *Kaloseidos (Beauty and Form)* showing the color scheme and a section of the design for the mural.

FIG. 57  Bacerra's mural *Kaloseidos (Beauty and Form)* (2003) installed at Western Asset Plaza, Pasadena. The mural measures 12 by 16 feet.

The exhibition *Great Pots: Contemporary Ceramics from Function to Fantasy* opens at the Newark Museum in New Jersey. It showcases a selection of the museum's permanent collection of modern and contemporary ceramics. Two of Bacerra's early porcelain plates with overglaze enamels

and metallic lusters are reproduced in the accompanying catalog: *Plate with Japanese Design* (1976) and *Large Bird Platter* (1986).[16]

## 2007–8

Bacerra's health is failing, but he continues working despite his increasing frailty. After months of uncertainty, he receives a definitive diagnosis of lung cancer. He rallies to finish the overglaze painting on his last large bowl and successfully accomplishes the task a few days before his death on June 10, 2008 (pp. 112–13).

FIG. 56  Announcement for the memorial celebrating the life of Ralph Bacerra, held at the Frank Lloyd Gallery, Bergamot Station, Santa Monica, July 27, 2008.

In 2008 *Art Is What I Do: The Life of Ralph Bacerra*, an Otis Legacy Project, is released and made accessible online. The twenty-seven-minute film contains interviews with family, friends, colleagues, and former students who shared their recollections of Bacerra.[17]

## 2015

The exhibition *Ralph Bacerra: Exquisite Beauty* is scheduled for presentation at Ben Maltz Gallery, Otis College of Art and Design, from September 26 to December 6.

Ceci n'est pas une pipe.

## NOTES

**1.** Ralph Bacerra, in filmed interview for the exhibition *Color and Fire: Defining Moments in Studio Ceramics, 1950–2000,* directed and produced for the Los Angeles County Museum of Art by Elvin Whitesides, Jo Lauria, and Megan Mellby; executive producer, Jane Burrell (2000).

**2.** Peter Shire, in *Art Is What I Do: The Life of Ralph Bacerra,* directed by Jo Lauria and produced by the Boardman Family Foundation in cooperation with Otis College of Art and Design (2008), Vimeo video, 25:50, posted by Otis College of Art and Design, 2014, https://vimeo.com/90053300.

**3.** Oral history interview with Ralph Bacerra, conducted by Frank Lloyd, April 7–19, 2004, Archives of American Art, Smithsonian Institution. It should be noted that in the interview Bacerra incorrectly remembered the date of Hamada's visit to USC as 1961, when in fact it was 1963. (Bacerra did correctly date the drawing he did of Hamada during the workshop as September 1963; see p. 30.) The visit is noted in the chronology of a book on Hamada: "1963: Exhibition with Leach in Paris; Attended the Second United States-Japan Conference on Cultural and Educational Interchange; Lectured at San Jose, Washington and Southern California universities." Atsushi Suzuki, *Tōshō Hamada Shōji: Jibun sagashi no etoranze* (Tokyo: Insatsu Iida Kyōdō Insatsu Kabushiki Kaisha, Heisei 7, 1995), 320.

**4.** The receipt is in the archives of the Ralph Bacerra Estate.

**5.** Peter Shire, e-mail correspondence with the author, May 31, 2015.

**6.** John Kimmelman (electrical engineer who worked for Ron Cunningham and Fasar), telephone conversation with the author, April 26, 2015.

**7.** Ken Deavers, in *Art Is What I Do.*

**8.** Lin Werner, conversation with the author, December 9, 2014.

**9.** Garth Clark and Mark Del Vecchio, e-mail correspondence with the author, May 30, 2015.

**10.** Garth Clark, *American Ceramics, 1876 to the Present* (New York: Abbeville, 1987), 254.

**11.** Elaine Levin, *The History of American Ceramics, 1607 to the Present: From Pipkins and Bean Pots to Contemporary Forms* (New York: Abrams, 1988), 332.

**12.** Frank Lloyd, e-mail correspondence with the author, April 29, 2015.

**13.** Garth Clark and Mark Del Vecchio, e-mail correspondence with the author, May 30, 2015.

**14.** See note 1 above.

**15.** Garth Clark, *The Artful Teapot* (New York: Watson-Guptill, 2001), 58.

**16.** Ulysses G. Dietz, *Great Pots: Contemporary Ceramics from Function to Fantasy* (Madison, WI: Guild, 2003), 11, 63.

**17.** See note 2 above.

Bacerra's worktable at his Eagle Rock studio, 2008. The large bowl on the banding wheel is the last ceramic piece he worked on before his death.

**Ralph Bacerra**, *Untitled Teapot*, 2001. Earthenware. 20½ × 14 × 16½ in. (52.1 × 35.6 × 41.9 cm). Collection of Sonny and Gloria Kamm.

Right: **Ralph Bacerra**, *Untitled Platter*, 2007 (detail). Ceramic. Height: 4 in. (10.2 cm); diameter: 28¼ in. (71.8 cm). Collection of David and Julianne Armstrong.

# Remembering Ralph Bacerra

This selection of personal writings about Ralph Bacerra includes remembrances written in response to his passing on June 10, 2008, and as well as more recent tributes to his memorable life. Bacerra's longtime gallery representative, Garth Clark, and the ceramist Don Pilcher, a former student of Bacerra's at Chouinard, originally published versions of the texts reprinted here in the journals *Ceramics Monthly* and the *Studio Potter*, respectively. Bacerra's former Los Angeles dealer Frank Lloyd wrote and delivered his eulogy on the occasion of the memorial gathering for the artist at the Frank Lloyd Gallery on July 27, 2008. The historian of ceramics Elaine Levin and the collector Keith Miller composed new texts for this publication. Collectively the writers present multiple perspectives on the artist and his career.—JL

## GARTH CLARK

Ralph Bacerra represented the pinnacle of a certain approach to ceramics that is no longer in vogue and, indeed, has not been for some years. He was unapologetically a decorative artist, and his muses were the potters who centuries ago decorated Japanese palace wares of Kutani, Nabeshima, and Imari, with their masterful use of surface decoration, often inspired by fabric designs. His fine arts affinities tended toward optical systems and stylization, a mix of M. C. Escher (without his mechanistic elements) with a dash of Warhol. His pots are technical and visual marvels and so superbly constructed and lusciously sensual. They went through multiple overglaze firings, with the temperature steadily reduced as each new layer was applied. This process is slow

and complex, and because of the many firings and Bacerra's love of technically challenging forms, the loss rate was high, painfully so, sometimes as much as 50 percent. But the results were worth it: hedonistic color, extravagant patterning, and optically complex surfaces.

The decoration process began with rudimentary sketching of the general surface scheme. After he bisque-fired one of his vessels, he would draw the complex decoration in pencil on the unglazed vessel. In the next firing, the second of what might be ten or more trips to the kiln, the pencil marks would of course vaporize. But he would remember the patterned interlocking schematic not just for that pot but also simultaneously for the ten to twenty others in that series on which he would also be working.

Bacerra's remarkable photographic memory was backed by an uncanny ability to measure volumetric space. He would show this off by announcing that he would make a vessel that would, when fired, contain a specific measure of water. The shape would often be new and complex, not just a cylinder. After the firing, it would then be tested and would hold exactly the amount of water he had projected.

The work reflects the man, one who had a paper-thin tolerance for any form of pretension. So his pots have no secret meanings. They carry no messages. They are not deconstructivist except accidentally so in the kiln. Bacerra described his goals modestly and unfashionably. In a 1994 interview published in *Ceramics: Art and Perception*, he commented, "I am not making any statements—social, political, conceptual, or even intellectual. There is no meaning or metaphor. I am committed more to the idea of pure beauty. When it is finished, the piece should be like an ornament, exquisitely beautiful."

His pieces celebrate thousands of years of decorative pottery, and yet, even though they are not instruments of intellectual inquiry, they are intelligent objects, alive with visual acuity. His adept craftsmanship is just what my partner, Mark Del Vecchio, and I came to expect of him. It was simply "what he did." It kept getting better, and we accepted that as well without much comment. Now, no matter how much we admire Bacerra's work, we are acutely aware of what we have lost after his death, and it's more than we realized. Simply stated, we have lost the most extraordinary decorative potter of the last fifty years. Initially I was hesitant to make this claim so boldly, but the more I thought

about it, the more I realized that it was an unassailable statement. Yes, America has produced many masters of decoration in the past half century. But it is no insult to any of them to say that his vast, multifaceted oeuvre stands in a class alone.

Bacerra was also one of the outstanding and most effective educators of the post–World War II period. He enjoyed teaching as much as making art, and the two were often in conflict. Actually, *enjoyed* is a poor choice of language; he absolutely adored the interchange between teacher and student. His own arts education began at what is now Orange Coast College in Costa Mesa, California, and he later transferred to the Chouinard Art Institute in Los Angeles, where he began his studies in ceramics.

Bacerra earned his BFA in 1961, then spent two years in the army. In 1963, after his discharge, he had just opened his own studio when he was invited to return to Chouinard as a tenured teacher. A year later he was appointed chair of the ceramics department. The Chouinard Art Institute's real importance, art historically speaking, comes from Bacerra's period of involvement. He insisted on a structured program with formal student critiques. At a time when education was becoming increasingly casual, he ensured that his students had a strong foundation of technical knowledge, particularly in glaze formulation. Students were encouraged to see technique as something more than science. They developed an appreciation for high craft as an "edge" that, if pushed far and intelligently enough, imparted tension, character, and content to the work. It took a while for the ideas that developed at Chouinard to jell, but by the mid-1970s Bacerra and his students Adrian Saxe, Don Pilcher, Mineo Mizuno, Peter Shire, Elsa Rady, and others had evolved an aesthetic that, while not homogeneous, did have many characteristics in common. All used ceramic with finesse, material richness, and a love of color. It was distinctive, stylish, and dynamic work, quintessentially Southern Californian art. Without knowing it at the time, they were the first of the postmodernists in ceramics.

The department closed when Chouinard became part of California Institute of the Arts and moved to a new campus outside Los Angeles. Bacerra did not teach formally again until 1982, when Otis Art Institute invited him to teach a glaze technology class. In 1983 he was asked to head the ceramics department at Otis, founded by Peter

Voulkos in 1954. He accepted the post not because he needed the income but because he so missed the camaraderie of teaching. He was an instant magnet for students, who were drawn by a complementary mix of generosity of spirit and exacting standards.

He remained there for fourteen years, and once again a group of successful, motivated, and productive students emerged: Cindy Kolodziejski, Diego Romero, Joan Takayama-Ogawa, Porntip Sangvanich, and many others, including Jo Lauria, who became a curator and writer on ceramics. This department closed in 1996. Otis was in the grip of a strictly conceptualist regime, and the fine arts chair objected to the fact that what Bacerra and his students did was, in her words, "too real." Happily, a different administration is now involved and has created a documentary and visual archive on Bacerra as part of the school's Otis Legacy Project, a program formed to record the oral history of outstanding Otis alumni.

While the prize of a major retrospective eluded Bacerra in his lifetime (as it does too many of our greats), he did get attention from the art world. The *New York Times* critic Ken Johnson—writing about one of the many exhibitions of Bacerra's work that Garth Clark Gallery organized between 1981 and 2006 (Ralph was one of the original twelve artists the gallery began with and continued to work with until we closed in 2006)—liked what he saw despite its lack of artspeak. "To look at [Bacerra's] gorgeous ceramic vessels," he wrote approvingly, "is to wallow in visual hedonism." Johnson added a remark that Bacerra loved (and that was doubly ironic given the reason for his departure from Otis), saying that conceptual art would be better off today if it could incorporate some of Bacerra's sensuality.

The *Los Angeles Times* writer William Wilson got it all wrong, however, describing Bacerra's set of cloud vessels as "ornate acts of visual prestidigitation that reduce the idea of opulence to a joke." The opulence of Bacerra's work was not a "joke" or any other self-conscious, self-loathing, postmodern contrivance, designed to worm around the difficult status of beauty in art today. Beauty for Bacerra was an unashamed reality, the ultimate level of visual success. It was why he made ceramics. He sought to contain the exquisite. I can only imagine how much he must have disliked Wilson's words.

Bacerra's social ethos was best captured in one of his last comments, made to Joan Takayama-Ogawa: "The joy in life is working in the studio, cooking, going out to eat good food and visiting with friends." He left two things off the list. One was laughter. Even though he could be cantankerous at times (our affectionate nickname for him at the gallery was Uncle Grumpy), he was never more than a twinkly eye away from bursting out with infectious laughter. Dinners at his home, aside from their high culinary achievement, were always distinguished by knee-weakening hilarity.

The other omission was his passion for growing orchids. Bacerra had a large greenhouse attached to the house and for years grew some of the rarest plants in the orchidaceous family. One night after dinner, I accompanied him and Atsuko Koyanagi, a leading Tokyo art dealer, on a tour of this collection. He stopped next to a particularly impressive bloom and announced that we were witnessing a special occasion because this orchid's flower appeared only once every five years. Without another word he plucked the flower from the stem and pinned it to Koyanagi's jacket. She stood overwhelmed by the gesture while Bacerra turned shyly away and gruffly changed the subject, lest the world discover that Uncle Grumpy, the unrelenting pragmatist, was at heart a closet romantic.

When Mark Del Vecchio and I spoke to Bacerra of his "art," he would argue that it was nothing more than good craft with some science thrown in for good effect. But what Bacerra achieved bordered on the magic of alchemy.

Ralph Bacerra passed away on June 10, 2008, at the age of seventy, succumbing to lung cancer. Although toward the end he had lost some of his sight and coordination, he completed a final piece just days before he died. He used a magnifying glass attached to his glasses in order to see well enough to complete the last of the multilayered china paint, then arranged for it to be fired two days before he passed away so that his dealer, Frank Lloyd, could deliver it to a client who had commissioned the piece. It was pure Bacerra: as reliable, disciplined, and responsible an artist as I have known. And Ralph was a very dear friend whom I had known since 1976 and whom I miss to this day.

## ELAINE LEVIN

I met Ralph in 1976, when I was asked by *Ceramics Monthly* magazine to write about his work. Others have discussed in detail his ceramics and his contributions to the field, with which I heartily concur. Here I'm confining myself to our relationship due to my writing and teaching about American ceramic history.

Ralph was on my list of Los Angeles–area ceramists, but I knew nothing about his work. I made an appointment to meet him at his home and studio in Eagle Rock. This small community between East Los Angeles and Pasadena is named for a dome-like geological out-cropping visible from Ralph's backyard patio.

Welcoming but shy (or cautious?) and apparently unaccustomed to talking about his work, Ralph nevertheless toured me around his home, studio, and patio. Work in progress and completed dinnerware, plat-ters, tureens, jars, vases, nested boxes, and sculptures crowded almost all the shelves and counters in his small cottage-like house. As amaz-ing as that display was to my early venture into writing about ceramic artists, I was equally fascinated by what seemed like every succulent and cactus known to botanists covering tables and makeshift surfaces in Ralph's backyard patio. My own beginning collection of this hardy plant life suddenly looked lackluster, definitely not in containers thrown and decorated by this innovative artist to complement each individual form.

Although I was aware of the interest in historical Japanese and Chinese ceramics by some Los Angeles ceramists, Ralph's interpreta-tion was unique. Asking about the reason for this direction as a major influence on his work, he explained how Vivika and Otto Heino, his teachers at Chouinard Art Institute in the 1960s, encouraged exploring the finest technical achievements of past cultures. Especially appealing to Ralph was gaining an understanding of the composition of clays, glazes, and design elements of Chinese Sung and Ming dynasty ceram-ics and Japanese Imari ware. Ralph's obvious love of intricate patterns placed his functional ware beyond the usual and familiar designs.

Among these designs was a mesmerizing blue dragon image on an off-white surface happily dancing around the interior of a large, low bowl.

Besides functional ware, Ralph showed me a four-legged, three-foot-high sculpture with a noticeable hump on its back. I did not understand how this creature fit into his aesthetic direction until later, when I crammed books on Chinese Tang dynasty ceramics and found the ubiquitous elegant Bactrian camels.

Another unexpected aspect of his ceramics at this time in this rather crowded environment was a stove tile. A friend's development of the Fasar stove, using electromagnetic induction instead of gas or electricity for heat, required a tile surface. Ralph had spent six months experimenting with formulas for a clay body that would not crack over radiated heat. This type of stove related also to Ralph's interest in food preparation and cooking. He had learned the culinary arts and especially Filipino dishes from his father, who had emigrated from the Philippines to the United States in the 1930s.

My article on Ralph's ceramics, succulents, and tiles was pub-lished in the April 1977 issue of the magazine. Meanwhile, Ralph, who had taught ceramics at Chouinard for eight years, ending in 1971, returned to academia. In 1982 he reinvigorated the ceramics depart-ment at Otis Art Institute. At that point I was teaching an experimental class on American ceramic history in the extension department of the University of California, Los Angeles (UCLA). Ralph asked me to teach that class for one semester at Otis. Thanks to Ralph, I spent one semes-ter a year for the next twelve years teaching at Otis and getting to know Ralph and a wonderful group of students.

The reserved Ralph I had met six years earlier, now a ceramics professor, had transformed (for me at least) into a much more affable person. I would look in on his classes after I finished teaching. He obviously loved interacting with his students, many also my students. Discussions about clay technology would often drift into someone's cooking experiment or dining at a local ethnic restaurant or the group's recent tour of a ceramics exhibition. I was included and much

enjoyed Ralph's cheery sense of humor and the comfortable teacher-student camaraderie.

I was writing a book on American ceramic history for use in my classes, not only at Otis but now also in the ceramics department at UCLA. I needed updated information from Ralph along with slides and photos of his recent ceramics. This time we met at his new, spacious, architecturally attractive hilltop home. A larger studio permitted him increasingly complex surface designs and forms. Recently, newly available china paints had attracted his exploratory nature. Remarkably, he had been rejected from joining an all-ladies china-painting class to learn the technique. Ralph-like, he proceeded to teach himself. Also, not content with extraordinary cactus plants, and now with more space,

Ralph had begun a burgeoning exotic orchid collection. Once again, his wide-ranging botanical interests and the functional ware that was now merging into sculptural dimensions captivated me.

We both left Otis in the mid-1990s. I saw an always gracious and welcoming Ralph intermittently at exhibition openings and ceramics groupie parties. Leaving the ceramics community at a much too early age, he nevertheless left a vital legacy. That legacy for me has been a number of his students (now professional ceramic artists) from his classes and mine at Otis. We've remained precious friends and colleagues, continuing to talk, laugh, and recall with pleasure special "Ralph moments."

**Ralph Bacerra**, *Teapot*, 1998. Porcelain. 7 × 7½ × 3¼ in. (17.8 × 19.1 × 8.3 cm). Collection of Lucille H. Epstein.

## FRANK LLOYD

Ralph Bacerra is celebrated as a true craftsman and a phenomenal artist. His work is in collections from the Smithsonian to the Victoria and Albert. The man we knew won our hearts by his loyalty, his consistency, and his thoughtful attention to his students. He was an avid gardener who cultivated exotic orchids, a traveler, a man who loved his dogs, and a gourmet cook. Ralph and his partner, Ron, cared deeply for each other. He was a brother, an uncle, and a teacher of hundreds. And Ralph just never seemed to age.

Yet what is fascinating, as we look back on this sudden loss, was his outlook on life. He had a singular vision—to be a ceramist. He told me about seeing a stoneware vessel in high school and learning about ceramics from Vivika Heino at Chouinard and how he had an immediate affinity for the medium. He was incredibly focused and directed from that time on. He became a leader in the movement of American studio ceramics, not just because of his generous talents but also because of his vision and hard work in the studio.

I once talked to a well-known art consultant about a commission for a large new building. I told her, "You should have Ralph do this, because he can do anything," and we know that he fulfilled the assignment. It is the monumental, three-thousand-piece tile commission for the Western Asset Plaza in Pasadena, which must be considered his masterpiece.

In a later conversation, an interview for the Archives of American Art, I asked Ralph to describe the difficulties or opportunities presented by that commission. He said, "Well, there weren't difficulties. I mean, if you know what you're doing and you have your vision. You have your idea, and it comes out. But all those things are sort of intuitive. You do research, you read books, you see the shows, and they're sort of in the back of your head, and as you begin to work, it all begins to come out. I think that most of the creativity comes from the actual doing—using your hands, using the clay, using the materials. And you can't sit there and think about it. My philosophy is you get in the studio and you get out the materials."

You may think that I am an art dealer, but actually I became a student of Ralph's. His questioning voice and his challenges were always there. When I stopped by his studio and brought his work to the gallery, he would tell me how it was made. When we traveled to San Francisco, he walked me through the collection of the Asian Art Museum and pointed out the prime examples. If my gallery showed new work, he came to test the ring of the pot and pronounced it properly fired—or not. I began to grasp the concepts of glaze "fit" and the order of firing.

It wasn't easy, but I guess I passed the tests. Because when Ralph took you on as a student, there was tremendous loyalty. He didn't let go. He was a true supporter of the gallery and never missed an opening— even the one three days before he died.

The amazing thing was how our relationship changed over the years. It began as a challenge to the newcomer and evolved into a student-teacher relationship, and then life intervened—and a friendship developed.

I learned that if I was sick Ralph would bring flowers in a vase he had made. He absolutely charmed my mother, who loved him and his work. We had things in common—the world of ceramics, a community of friends, and our houses in Eagle Rock.

Around two years ago we started to have breakfast every Sunday morning. Ralph was a disciplined and punctual man, so he always called right at the same time. I learned that it was better for him to drive because he was impatient with other people's driving. As we talked during our drive or at breakfast, I learned what meant the most to Ralph.

For Ralph, the important things during the later years were simple: working in the studio, the pursuit of beauty, the company of friends, and . . . a meal together.

Opposite, top: **Ralph Bacerra**, *Untitled Round Lidded Vessel*, c. 1979. Ceramic. Height: 7½ in. (19 cm); diameter: 11 in. (27.9 cm). Collection of George and Connie Bacerra.

Opposite, bottom: **Ralph Bacerra**, *Covered Vessel*, c. 1979. Porcelain. Height: 9 in. (22.9 cm); diameter: 15 in. (38.1 cm). Private collection.

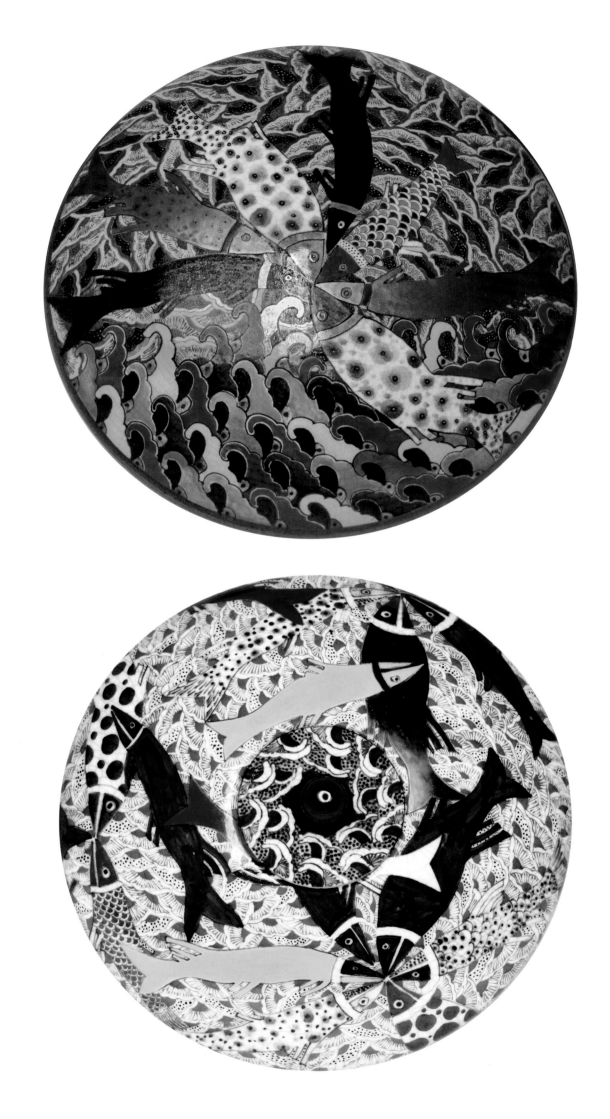

## KEITH MILLER

When Peter Voulkos and Rudy Autio loaded abstract expressionism onto a pickup truck and drove it to Montana, they replaced centuries of ceramic tradition with a rude spontaneity. Meanwhile Shōji Hamada and Kanjirō Kawai climbed into a time machine to revisit age-old folk pottery in Japan. These two journeys might not be quite as different as they appear: the expressivist ceramist Don Reitz, a wizard of firing, once told me that he sometimes intentionally created effects that he made look accidental. Still, Voulkos's large battered sculptures are a long way from Hamada's vivacious but humble tableware.

Enter Ralph Bacerra. He adored the incredible technical achievements of Japanese Imari ware from the eighteenth and nineteenth centuries and understood how Imari artists built on eons of stunning accomplishments by East Asian potters. Yet Bacerra was also an American modernist who engaged cubism and color-field abstraction. Through some form of alchemy unknown to others, he managed to yoke the opposites of open rebellion and cherished tradition. His works sprang from a vast knowledge of East Asian glazes and from his own countless scientific glaze experiments. Yet his designs also dialogue with the impossible perspectives of M. C. Escher and the bright non-Euclidean geometries of Al Held.

Bacerra's mutually eclipsing, always sliding checkerboards and optically illusionist staircases bewitch the eye while simultaneously upholding and defying two-dimensional space. His stark modernity critiques many well-rehearsed rituals in clay. Yet his respectful reinvention of age-old practices—particularly in glazing—rebukes those modern artists who seek the easy path of discarding everything before the Armory Show. He seized immense artistic resources of the past in order to assert a dizzying present. I can't imagine twentieth-century art without Ralph Bacerra, and neither should anyone else.

## DON PILCHER

To call Ralph Bacerra a studio potter is to expand the definition to include the maker of some of the most complex, opulent, and ambitious pottery ever created. His death at home this past June from lung cancer brings an end to one of the most productive lives many of us have ever witnessed.

Ralph was a very private man, not given to expansive explanation or audible conjecture. I don't know that I ever heard him speak four consecutive sentences. And yet he was a warm, engaging, even intimate person. He achieved this by frequently addressing you by name, listening carefully, and making modest yet intense eye contact, his chin down but his eyes locked on yours. He was also a generous man—generous with his knowledge, personal influence, and treasure. He took quiet delight in giving his students a professional boost, usually claiming that he did no such thing. He had a fine sense of humor and ready laugh. And no one was quicker to pick up the check at lunch. In his own right, he was a great cook, and when the food came to the table, the pots and pans had already been done—more time for conversation.

But Ralph was not everyman. By most standards, he had considerable wealth but used it judiciously. He did not suffer fools. He was ferociously talented, professionally proud, personally modest, a man of conviction bordering on stubbornness, movie-star handsome, and genetically predisposed to produce fabulous pottery at the intersection of Memphis and Imari. He had perfect recall for all things ceramic. If asked about a glaze, he would say, "Well, Don, it's just the celadon with extra silica," seemingly a little disappointed that I didn't know that.

To the dismay of interviewers, he never had a great deal to say about his ceramics other than expressing his desire for beauty. But we can surmise volumes by a careful look at the body of work he leaves behind. That potent collection illustrates Ralph's formalist belief that animated and colorful geometry, lyrically composed and repeated with infinite variety, could and would stimulate the eye, entertain the mind,

and revive the spirit. Ralph made this beauty distinctive through the exponential power of his execution. His multiple applications, whether by brush or otherwise, were lavish not slavish. And unlike most potters of any recent generation, he understood the difference between refiring to fix a problem and refiring to create an aggregate aesthetic. Really, who else do you know who regularly fires each work a minimum of twelve times?

Of singular importance was Ralph's genius for imaginative and expansive reciprocating compositions. He was a master of the dance of two shapes, wherein each yields in turn to the necessity of the other. He intuitively knew how many *shorts* satisfied a *long*, how much *in* was required by this *out* and how much *curve* energized this *angle*. He was Fibonacci incarnate. Nobody could prestidigitate simple geometry with greater élan or less apparent effort. (Speaking of less apparent effort, you shouldn't be surprised to know that he never got clay or glaze on anything but his apron, that his working jeans always had a crease, and that he never cursed.)

So what can we take away from this man's work? In addition to their beauty, Ralph's pots demonstrate and even proselytize for a greater commitment to our collective art form. He found work to be life affirming, and by Garth Clark's account, he was finishing a few pieces just two days before he died. By Ralph's example we are shown, if not shamed into rethinking, what is possible when we apply every gift we have with all our heart.

When I last saw him in January, we spent most of the day talking families, art, schools, and the future. He was deeply concerned that so much of the ceramic field had apparently turned its back on teaching superb hand skills and deep technical knowledge and inculcating a rigorous work ethic. His question was "Where do they think this will take them?" Where indeed.

Opposite: **Ralph Bacerra**, *Untitled Teapot*, 2005.
Ceramic. 7½ × 16 × 8 in. (19.1 × 40.6 × 20.3 cm).
Collection of Alan Mandell.

Opposite, top: **Ralph Bacerra**, *Yellow Cup and Saucer*,
1993. Ceramic. 3 × 6½ × 6 in. (7.6 × 16.5 × 15.2 cm).

Opposite, bottom: **Ralph Bacerra**, *Turquoise Cup and
Saucer*, 1993. Ceramic. 3 × 6½ × 6 in. (7.6 × 16.5 × 15.2 cm).

Above: **Ralph Bacerra**, *Untitled Cup and Saucer*, 1990.
Glazed porcelain. Cup: 4 × 4¾ × 5¼ in. (10.2 × 12.1 × 13.3
cm); saucer: height: ¾ in. (1.9 cm); diameter: 6¼ in. (15.9
cm). Collection of Karen Smits.

# Works in the Exhibition

*Untitled Vessel*, c. 1968–69
Stoneware
Height: 23 in. (58.4 cm); diameter:
14 in. (35.6 cm)
Collection of Porntip Sangvanich

*Untitled Covered Jar*, 1969
Glazed stoneware
Height: 18 in. (45.7 cm); diameter:
13 in. (33 cm)
Collection of Peter and Cindy Bass/
Cindy Lee Bass, Executor of the
Ralph Bacerra Estate
**PAGE 33**

*Nefertiti*, c. 1972
Ceramic
22 × 7½ × 7 in. (55.9 × 19.1 × 17.8 cm)
Collection of Ava Shire
**PAGE 47**

*Untitled Sculpture*, 1972
Ceramic
39½ × 16 × 12 in. (100.3 × 40.6 ×
30.5 cm)
Collection of George and
Connie Bacerra
**PAGE 85**

*Green Casserole*, c. 1973
Stoneware
Lid: height: 3 in. (7.6 cm); diameter:
11 in. (27.9 cm)
Base: height: 5¾ in. (14.6 cm);
diameter: 11 in. (27.9 cm)
Long Beach Museum of Art, Long
Beach, CA, Gift of Garth Clark and
Mark Del Vecchio
**PAGE 18**

*Covered Vessel with Handles*, 1975
Porcelain
Height: 15 in. (38.1 cm); diameter:
9½ in. (24.1 cm)
Collection of Ken Deavers
**PAGE 18**

*Dragon Platter*, c. 1975
Porcelain
1 × 14 × 7½ in. (2.5 × 35.6 × 19.1 cm)
Collection of Lin Werner
**PAGE 33**

*Untitled Animal Form*, c. 1976
Ceramic
34¾ × 35⅞ × 16⅝ in. (88.3 × 91.1 ×
42.2 cm)
Collection of Forrest L. Merrill
**PAGE 67**

*Untitled Animal Form*, c. 1976
Ceramic
33 × 41¼ × 10 in. (83.8 × 104.8 ×
25.4 cm)
Collection of Forrest L. Merrill
**PAGE 59**

*Stacking Porcelain Bowls*, c. 1977
Porcelain
Height: 7¼ in. (18.4 cm); diameter:
6¾ in. (17.1 cm)
American Museum of Ceramic Art,
Gift of James W. and Jackie Voell,
2005.2.0031
**PAGE 97**

*Untitled Stacking Covered Vessel*,
1977
Porcelain
Height: 13 in. (33 cm); diameter:
6½ in. (16.5 cm)
Collection of Susan Steinhauser and
Dan Greenberg
**PAGE 23**

*Iris Platter*, c. 1978
White stoneware
1 × 16 × 10 in. (2.5 × 40.6 × 25.4 cm)
Collection of Lin Werner
**PAGE 39**

*Covered Vessel*, c. 1979
Porcelain
Height: 9 in. (22.9 cm); diameter:
15 in. (38.1 cm)
Private collection
**PAGE 121**

*Untitled Round Lidded Vessel*, c. 1979
Ceramic
Height: 7½ in. (19 cm); diameter:
11 in. (27.9 cm)
Collection of George and
Connie Bacerra
**PAGE 121**

*Untitled Plates: Set of Four*,
c. late 1970s
Ceramic
Height: 2 in. (5.1 cm); diameter: 12 in.
(30.5 cm) each
Collection of Peter and Cindy Bass/
Cindy Lee Bass, Executor of the
Ralph Bacerra Estate

*Study of Birds*, c. 1980
Gouache on paper
18 × 24 in. (45.7 × 61 cm)
Collection of Peter and Cindy Bass/
Cindy Lee Bass, Executor of the
Ralph Bacerra Estate
**PAGE 32**

*Test Plate for Overglaze Enamels*,
c. early 1980s
Ceramic
Height: 1 in. (2.5 cm); diameter: 12 in.
(30.5 cm)
Collection of Peter and Cindy Bass/
Cindy Lee Bass, Executor of the
Ralph Bacerra Estate
**PAGE 98**

*Untitled Cup*, c. early 1980s
Porcelain
5 × 4 × 4 in. (12.7 × 10.2 × 10.2 cm)
Collection of Lin Werner

*Untitled Dinner Plate*, c. early 1980s
Ceramic
Height: 1 in. (2.5 cm); diameter: 12 in.
(30.5 cm)
Collection of Peter and Cindy Bass/
Cindy Lee Bass, Executor of the
Ralph Bacerra Estate
**PAGE 98**

*Untitled Covered Vessel*, c. 1980s
Porcelain
Height: 12 in. (30.5 cm); diameter:
15 in. (38.1 cm)
Collection of Peter and Cindy Bass/
Cindy Lee Bass, Executor of the
Ralph Bacerra Estate
**PAGE 58**

*Untitled Platter*, c. 1980s
Ceramic
2 × 12 × 7 in. (5.1 × 30.5 × 17.8 cm)
Collection of Peter and Cindy Bass/
Cindy Lee Bass, Executor of the
Ralph Bacerra Estate
**PAGE 54**

*Untitled Platter*, c. 1980s
Ceramic
2 × 12 × 7¼ in. (5.1 × 30.5 × 18.4 cm)
Collection of Peter and Cindy Bass/
Cindy Lee Bass, Executor of the
Ralph Bacerra Estate
**PAGE 54**

*Untitled Platter*, c. 1980s
Ceramic
2¼ × 19½ × 16 in. (2.3 × 49.5 ×
40.6 cm)
Collection of Peter and Cindy Bass/
Cindy Lee Bass, Executor of the
Ralph Bacerra Estate

*Untitled Platter*, c. 1980s
Stoneware
3 × 16 × 11 in. (7.6 × 40.6 × 27.9 cm)
Collection of Peter and Cindy Bass/
Cindy Lee Bass, Executor of the
Ralph Bacerra Estate
**PAGE 99**

*Untitled Platter with Handle*, c. 1980s
Stoneware
8 × 13 × 13 in. (20.3 × 33 × 33 cm)
Collection of Peter and Cindy Bass/
Cindy Lee Bass, Executor of the
Ralph Bacerra Estate

*Untitled Platter with Handle*, c. 1980s
Stoneware
1½ × 12½ × 7½ in. (3.8 × 31.8 ×
19.1 cm)
Collection of Porntip Sangvanich
**PAGE 100**

*Untitled Platter*, 1982
Porcelain
Height: 3 in. (7.6 cm); diameter:
19 in. (48.3 cm)
Collection of Ted Rowland
**PAGE 19**

*Blue Cup*, 1983
Ceramic
3½ × 6 × 3 in. (8.9 × 15.2 × 7.6 cm)
Collection of Lucille H. Epstein

*Interlocking Bird Wall Relief*, 1983
Ceramic
36 × 33 × 3 in. (91.4 × 83.8 × 7.6 cm)
Collection of George and
Connie Bacerra
**PAGE 130**

*Untitled Cup with Triangles*, 1983
Ceramic
3½ × 6¼ × 3 in. (8.9 × 15.9 × 7.6 cm)
Collection of Peter and Cindy Bass/
Cindy Lee Bass, Executor of the
Ralph Bacerra Estate

*Untitled Wall Mural*, 1983
Ceramic
27½ × 29½ × 3 in. (69.9 × 74.9 ×
7.6 cm)
Collection of Karen Smits

*Untitled Platter*, 1984
Ceramic
3 × 25 × 18 in. (7.6 × 63.5 × 45.7 cm)
Collection of Alan Mandell
**PAGE 104**

*Untitled Platter*, 1986
Earthenware with underglaze, glaze,
and overglaze painting
Height: 3⅜ in. (8.6 cm); diameter:
23 in. (58.4 cm)
Collection of Garth Clark and
Mark Del Vecchio
**PAGE 103**

*Untitled Twig Cup*, 1986
Glazed porcelain
3¼ × 3¼ × 5 in. (8.3 × 8.3 × 12.7 cm)
Collection of Karen Smits

*Untitled Platter*, 1988
Earthenware with underglaze, glaze,
and overglaze painting
3½ × 24 × 24 in. (8.9 × 61 × 61 cm).
Collection of Bronya and Andy Galef
**PAGE 53**

*Vessel/Violet*, 1988
Glazed earthenware with lusters
11½ × 22 × 22 in. (29.2 × 55.9 ×
55.9 cm)
Arizona State University Art Museum;
Museum purchase through a gift
from the Stéphane Janssen Art
Foundation
**PAGE 28**

*Teapot*, 1989
Ceramic
17 × 12 × 8½ in. (43.2 × 30.5 ×
21.6 cm)
Collection of Lucille H. Epstein
**PAGE 70**

*Untitled Stacking Box*, c. late 1980s
Porcelain, overglaze enamel, and
metallic luster
Height: 12 in. (30.5 cm); diameter:
5 in. (12.7 cm)
Collection of Lin Werner
**PAGE 134**

*Set of Four Demonstration China-
Painting Plates*, c. 1990
Ceramic
Height: 1 in. (2.5 cm); diameter: 12 in.
(30.5 cm) each
Collection of Forrest L. Merrill
**PAGES 40–41**

*Untitled Cup and Saucer*, 1990
Glazed porcelain
Cup: 4 × 4¾ × 5¼ in. (10.2 × 12.1 ×
13.3 cm)
Saucer: height: ¾ in. (1.9 cm);
diameter: 6¼ in. (15.9 cm)
Collection of Karen Smits
**PAGE 125**

*Gold Cup*, 1991
Ceramic
8 × 4½ × 3½ in. (20.3 × 11.4 ×
8.9 cm)
Private collection
**PAGE 1**

*Portrait Vessel*, 1991
Whiteware
25 × 22 × 4¾ in. (63.5 × 55.9 ×
12.1 cm)
Arizona State University Art
Museum; Gift of Anne and
Sam Davis
**PAGE 42**

*Turquoise Cup and Saucer*, 1993
Ceramic
3 × 6½ × 6 in. (7.6 × 16.5 × 15.2 cm)
Collection of Peter and Cindy Bass/
Cindy Lee Bass, Executor of the
Ralph Bacerra Estate
**PAGE 124**

*Untitled Portrait Charger*, 1993
Ceramic
7⅝ × 25¾ × 25 in.
(19.4 × 65.4 × 63.5 cm)
Collection of Anne Cohen
Ruderman and David Ruderman
**PAGE 21**

*Yellow Cup and Saucer*, 1993
Ceramic
3 × 6½ × 6 in. (7.6 × 16.5 × 15.2 cm)
Collection of Peter and Cindy Bass/
Cindy Lee Bass, Executor of the
Ralph Bacerra Estate
**PAGE 124**

*Pink Cup with Stepped Handle*, 1994
Ceramic
3 × 6 × 3 in. (7.6 × 15.2 × 7.6 cm)
Collection of Lucille H. Epstein

*Untitled Female Figure/Tang*, 1994
Whiteware
29 × 10 × 7 in. (73.7 × 25.4 × 17.8 cm)
Collection of Patti and Mike Marcus
**PAGE 86**

*Cup with Branch Handle*, 1996
Ceramic
4 × 4 × 5 in. (10.2 × 10.2 × 12.7 cm)
Collection of Lucille H. Epstein

*Double Portrait*, 1996
Porcelain
Height: 9 in. (22.9 cm); diameter:
15 in. (38.1 cm)
Private collection
**PAGE 65**

*Pair of Copper Red Cups*, 1996
Ceramic
4 × 4½ × 4 in. (10.2 × 11.4 × 10.2 cm)
each
Collection of Sue Wilson Keane

*Untitled Pink Marbleized Cup*, 1996
Ceramic
3¾ × 5 × 4 in. (9.5 × 12.7 × 10.2 cm)
Collection of Peter and Cindy Bass/
Cindy Lee Bass, Executor of the
Ralph Bacerra Estate

*Covered Vessel*, 1997
Ceramic
7½ × 21 × 17 in. (19.1 × 53.3 × 43.2 cm)
Collection of Paul and Sharon Dauer
**PAGE 107**

*Untitled Cloud Vessel*, 1997
Porcelain
20½ × 13 × 6 in. (52.1 × 33 × 15.2 cm)
Collection of Saul E. Levi
**PAGE 63**

*Cloud Teapot*, 1998
Whiteware
21 × 20 × 5 in. (53.3 × 50.8 × 12.7 cm)
Collection of Alan Mandell
**PAGE 27**

*Teapot*, 1998
Porcelain
7 × 7½ × 3¼ in. (17.8 × 19.1 × 8.3 cm)
Collection of Lucille H. Epstein
**PAGE 119**

Untitled, 1998
Porcelain
15½ × 19½ × 17⅝ in. (39.4 × 49.5 ×
44.8 cm)
Collection of Forrest L. Merrill
**PAGES 2–3**

*Untitled Lidded Vessel*, 1998
Earthenware
29 × 17½ × 16 in. (73.7 × 44.5 ×
40.6 cm)
Collection of David and Julianne
Armstrong, Promised gift to the
American Museum of Ceramic Art
**PAGE 49**

*Untitled Teapot*, 1998
Earthenware
17 × 13 × 10 in. (43.2 × 33 × 25.4 cm)
Collection of Ken Deavers
**PAGE 20**

*Untitled Vessel*, 1999
Porcelain
20 × 15 × 8 in. (50.8 × 38.1 × 20.3 cm)
Collection of Alan Mandell
**PAGE 13**

*Untitled Dinnerware*, 1999–2000
Ceramic
**SOUP BOWL:** height: 2 in. (5.1 cm);
diameter: 7 in. (17.8 cm)
**TWO CUPS:** 3¾ × 4¾ × 5¼ in. (9.5 ×
12.1 × 13.3 cm) each
**TWO SAUCERS:** height: ¾ in. (1.9 cm);
diameter: 6¼ in. (15.9 cm) each
**TWO PLATES:** height: 1 in. (2.5 cm);
diameter: 9½ in. (24.1 cm) each
**CHARGER:** height: 1¼ in. (3.2 cm);
diameter: 13½ in. (34.3 cm)
Collection of Peter and Cindy Bass/
Cindy Lee Bass, Executor of the
Ralph Bacerra Estate

*Cloud Vessel*, 2000
Porcelain
22 × 14½ × 6 in. (55.9 × 36.8 ×
15.2 cm)
Collection of Paul and Sharon Dauer
**PAGE 50**

*Untitled Teapot/Coffeepot*, 2000
Ceramic
12 × 8 × 7 in. (30.5× 20.3 × 17.8 cm)
Collection of Peter and Cindy Bass/
Cindy Lee Bass, Executor of the
Ralph Bacerra Estate

*Untitled Gold Vessel*, 2001
Earthenware
Height: 31½ in. (80 cm); diameter:
22 in. (55.9 cm)
Collection of Peter and Cindy Bass/
Cindy Lee Bass, Executor of the
Ralph Bacerra Estate
**PAGE 109**

*Untitled Lidded Vessel*, 2001
Earthenware
32 × 16 × 9½ in. (81.3 × 40.6 ×
24.1 cm)
Collection of Peter and Cindy Bass/
Cindy Lee Bass, Executor of the
Ralph Bacerra Estate
**PAGE 61**

*Untitled Lidded Vessel*, 2001
Earthenware
31½ × 18½ × 13 in. (80 × 47 × 33 cm)
Collection of Peter and Cindy Bass/
Cindy Lee Bass, Executor of the
Ralph Bacerra Estate

*Untitled Teapot*, 2001
Earthenware
20½ × 14 × 16½ in. (52.1 × 35.6 ×
41.9 cm)
Collection of Sonny and
Gloria Kamm
**PAGE 114**

Untitled, 2002
Ceramic
Height: 23½ in. (59.7 cm); diameter:
8 in. (20.3 cm)
Collection of Dr. and Mrs. Terasaki
**PAGE 48**

Untitled, 2002
Ceramic
Height: 29 in. (73.7 cm); diameter:
14 in. (35.6 cm)
Collection of Lois and
Robert Boardman
**PAGE 68**

Rendering for *Kaloseidos (Beauty
and Form)*, 2003
Watercolor on paper
40 × 28 in. (101.6 × 71.1 cm) framed
Collection of Peter and Cindy Bass/
Cindy Lee Bass, Executor of the
Ralph Bacerra Estate
**PAGE 22**

*Tile Sample for Western Asset
Commission: Study for Mural*, 2003
Ceramic, wood frame
29¾ × 23½ × 1¼ in. (73.7 × 59.7 ×
3.2 cm) framed
Collection of Porntip Sangvanich
**PAGE 110**

Untitled, 2003
Whiteware
29 × 12 × 6 in. (73.7 × 30.5 ×
15.2 cm)
Collection of David and
Julianne Armstrong
**PAGE 69**

*Cartoon for Wall Art, New England
Biolabs*, 2004
Watercolor on paper
66 × 24 in. (167.6 × 60.1 cm)
Collection of Peter and Cindy Bass/
Cindy Lee Bass, Executor of the
Ralph Bacerra Estate

*Untitled Luster Cup with Base*, 2004
Ceramic
10 × 9⅛ × 6¾ in. (25.4 × 23.2 ×
17.1 cm)
Collection of Peter and Cindy Bass/
Cindy Lee Bass, Executor of the
Ralph Bacerra Estate

*Untitled Plate*, 2005
Ceramic
Height: 2 in. (5.1 cm); diameter: 22½
in. (57.2 cm)
Collection of Wendy Barrie
Brotman and David Brotman
**PAGE 136**

*Untitled Platter*, 2005
Ceramic
3½ × 24½ × 20½ in. (8.9 × 62.2 × 52.1 cm)
Collection of Alan Mandell

*Untitled Teapot*, 2005
Ceramic
17½ × 14½ × 10½ in. (44.5 × 36.8 × 26.7 cm)
Collection of Peter and Cindy Bass/
Cindy Lee Bass, Executor of the
Ralph Bacerra Estate
*Untitled Teapot*, 2005
Ceramic
7½ × 16 × 8 in. (19.1 × 40.6 × 20.3 cm)
Collection of Alan Mandell
**PAGE 122**

*Untitled Teapot*, 2005
Ceramic
20½ × 14 × 5½ in. (52.1 × 35.6 × 14 cm)
Collection of Mary Coquillard
**PAGE 87**

*Untitled White Swirl Cup*, 2005
Ceramic
3 × 5 × 3¼ in. (7.6 × 12.7 × 8.3 cm)
Collection of Peter and Cindy Bass/
Cindy Lee Bass, Executor of the
Ralph Bacerra Estate

*Untitled Turquoise Bowl*, 2006
Ceramic
Height: 14½ in. (36.8 cm); diameter:
25 in. (63.5 cm)
Collection of Peter and Cindy Bass/
Cindy Lee Bass, Executor of the
Ralph Bacerra Estate
**PAGE 43**

*Untitled Vessel*, 2006
Ceramic
27 × 15 × 8 in. (68.6 × 38.1 × 20.3 cm)
Collection of Peter and Cindy Bass/
Cindy Lee Bass, Executor of the
Ralph Bacerra Estate

*Untitled Platter*, 2007
Ceramic
Height: 4 in. (10.2 cm); diameter:
28¼ in. (71.8 cm)
Collection of David and
Julianne Armstrong
**PAGE 57**

*Untitled Platter*, 2007
Ceramic
Height: 4 in. (10.2 cm); diameter:
28¼ in. (71.8 cm)
Collection of David and
Julianne Armstrong
**PAGE 8**

*Untitled Platter*, 2007
Ceramic
Height: 4 in. (10.2 cm); diameter:
28¼ in. (71.8 cm)
Collection of David and
Julianne Armstrong
**PAGE 9**

*Untitled Platter*, 2007
Ceramic
Height: 4 in. (10.2 cm); diameter:
28¼ in. (71.8 cm)
Collection of Peter and Cindy Bass/
Cindy Lee Bass, Executor of the
Ralph Bacerra Estate
**PAGE 10**

*Untitled Bowl*, 2008
Ceramic
Height: 18½ in. (45.7 cm); diameter:
22 in. (55.9 cm)
Collection of Douglas Moreland
**PAGE 45**

*Teapot*, n.d.
Earthenware
20 × 12 × 17 in. (50.8 × 30.5 × 43.2 cm)
Collection of Sonny and
Gloria Kamm
**PAGE 26**

*Untitled Bowl*, n.d.
Ceramic
Height: 3 in. (7.6 cm); diameter: 5 in.
(12.7 cm)
Collection of Peter and Cindy Bass/
Cindy Lee Bass, Executor of the
Ralph Bacerra Estate
**PAGE 132**

*Untitled Bowl*, n.d.
Ceramic
Height: 3 in. (7.6 cm); diameter: 5 in.
(12.7 cm)
Collection of Peter and Cindy Bass/
Cindy Lee Bass, Executor of the
Ralph Bacerra Estate
**PAGE 133**

*Untitled Confetti Cup*, n.d.
Ceramic
3¼ × 4½ × 3¼ in. (8.3 × 11.4 × 8.3 cm)
Collection of Peter and Cindy Bass/
Cindy Lee Bass, Executor of the
Ralph Bacerra Estate

*Untitled Cup (Branch)*, n.d.
Earthenware
3½ × 5½ × 3½ in. (8.9 × 14 × 8.9 cm)
Collection of David and
Julianne Armstrong

*Untitled Cup with Gold*, n.d.
Ceramic
3½ × 5 × 3¼ in. (8.9 × 12.7 × 8.3 cm)
Collection of Peter and Cindy Bass/
Cindy Lee Bass, Executor of the
Ralph Bacerra Estate

*Untitled Cup with Incised Gold Accent*, n.d.
Ceramic
3½ × 5 × 3¾ in. (8.9 × 12.7 × 9.5 cm)
Collection of Peter and Cindy Bass/
Cindy Lee Bass, Executor of the
Ralph Bacerra Estate

*Untitled Lidded Box*, n.d.
Ceramic
3½ × 11 × 6 in. (8.9 × 27.9 × 15.2 cm)
Collection of Ted Rowland
**PAGE 56**

*Untitled Platter*, n.d.
Ceramic, porcelain
Height: 4 in. (10.2 cm); diameter:
19 in. (48.3 cm)
Collection of Peter and Cindy Bass/
Cindy Lee Bass, Executor of the
Ralph Bacerra Estate

*Untitled Platter*, n.d.
Ceramic, porcelain
Height: 4 in. (10.2 cm); diameter:
22 in. (55.9 cm)
Collection of Peter and Cindy Bass/
Cindy Lee Bass, Executor of the
Ralph Bacerra Estate

*Untitled Test Bowls*, n.d.
Ceramic
Height: 2¼ in. (5.7 cm); diameter:
6¼ in. (15.9 cm)
Height: 2 in. (5.1 cm); diameter: 5¾
in. (14.6 cm)
Height: 2¼ in. (5.7 cm); diameter:
4¾ in. (12.1 cm)
Height: 3 in. (7.6 cm); diameter: 6 in.
(15.2 cm)
Height: 2 in. (5.1 cm); diameter: 6 in.
(15.2 cm)
Height: 1¾ in. (4.4 cm); diameter:
4 in. (10.2 cm)
Height: 3 in. (7.6 cm); diameter: 6 in.
(15.2 cm)
Height: 2¾ in. (7 cm); diameter: 6 in.
(15.2 cm)
2 × 6¼ × 7 in. (5.1 × 15.9 × 17.8 cm)
2 × 7 × 5½ in. (5.1 × 17.8 × 14 cm)
2 × 6 × 7 in. (5.1 × 15.2 × 17.8 cm)
Collection of Peter and Cindy Bass/
Cindy Lee Bass, Executor of the
Ralph Bacerra Estate

**Ralph Bacerra**, *Interlocking Bird Wall Relief*, 1983. Ceramic.
36 × 33 × 3 in. (91.4 × 83.8 × 7.6 cm). Collection of George
and Connie Bacerra.

# Acknowledgments

The origination, development, and presentation of *Ralph Bacerra: Exquisite Beauty* have been an involved process spanning many years. Having completed graduate studies in ceramics with Ralph Bacerra in 1990, I could not have imagined that our paths would cross again at this juncture, but I am honored to have the opportunity to chronicle this important artist's life and work. Bacerra was underrecognized during his lifetime; as a curator and former student I felt a responsibility to acknowledge his significant accomplishments and contributions to the field. It is regrettable that this tribute is being presented posthumously; all who were touched by Bacerra's life would have preferred it otherwise. His death left much unfinished; it was an ill-timed end to an exceptional creative career.

Through intimate study of the Bacerra archives (courtesy of the Ralph Bacerra Estate) and personal interviews with close family, friends, and colleagues, I have come to know this artist deeply and to acquire a profound appreciation of his virtuosity—far beyond what I experienced as a student in the Otis ceramics studio. I feel privileged to have had access to the inner sanctum of Bacerra—to bear witness to the passion he expressed and the dedication he sustained in pursuit of his craft. I am grateful for the opportunity to widen the circle of exposure and appreciation of his artwork through this exhibition and publication and am indebted to the Otis trustees and board of governors and to the Ben Maltz Gallery staff for their commitment to this project from its inception and their confidence in its completion.

My first and most heartfelt thanks go to those who have supported and nurtured this endeavor every step of the way: Cindy Lee Bass, executor of the Ralph Bacerra Estate, who freely gave access to the Bacerra archives and provided invaluable assistance, advocacy, funding, and unflagging enthusiasm throughout. Lois Boardman, Joan Takayama-Ogawa, Porntip Sangvanich, and Lin Werner have become indefatigable pillars of support. I am deeply grateful for their wise council, financial support, and enduring friendship. To Meg Linton, former director of galleries and exhibitions at Otis, I offer my sincerest thanks for the vision, strength, and unwavering commitment to present Bacerra's work to the public. I express my deep appreciation to Frank Lloyd, founder of Frank Lloyd Gallery and adviser to this project, for his generosity of spirit and meticulous professionalism. I also extend my gratitude to the gallery's key staff, particularly Kelly Boyd, assistant director, and Gabriel Seri, assistant director. Anne Swett-Predock, Otis's creative director, designed dynamic exhibition graphics that match the exuberance of Bacerra's ceramics. The architect and installation designer Michael Patrick Porter contributed immeasurably to the public's understanding and appreciation of Bacerra and his work through the inspired exhibition design that he conceived and executed.

We are most grateful for the support we received from the National Endowment for the Arts, carrying along with it the affirmation of the worthiness of this undertaking. Further, an early and critically important grant from the Pasadena Art Alliance was instrumental in the research and production phase of this catalog. The Boardman Family Foundation underwrote additional publication costs, and educational programs were sponsored in part by grants from the Friends of Contemporary Ceramics and Japan Art Foundation, Los Angeles. To these generous funders we offer our sincere thanks. I am indebted to the numerous individual donors, many of them devoted alumni, who have liberally given financial support. Their names are listed on page 133.

The catalog was enhanced by the keen insights and rigorous scholarship of the contributing writers: Jeannine Falino, Hollis Goodall, and Christy Johnson. They have given voice to Bacerra's creative output and written incisive essays situating his work within the history of ceramics. Further, I offer my sincere appreciation to our editor, Karen Jacobson, for her thoughtful and sensitive response to the content of this catalog. I am extremely grateful to Amy McFarland, an award-winning designer and an Otis Outstanding Alumna in Communication Design, for the imaginative, innovative, and exquisitely beautiful design she created for this publication. I thank the many photographers whose talents made Bacerra's pieces shine on every page, notably David Peters, Anthony Cuñha, and M. Lee Fatherree. (We acknowledge all the photographers on page 6.)

Many Otis staff, faculty, and students have directly and enthusiastically supported this exhibition and catalog, and for their efforts I am profoundly thankful. The staff of the Ben Maltz Gallery is recognized on page 133. Additionally I'd like to acknowledge the efforts of others who generously gave of their time and expertise: Kerry Walk, interim president; Karen Moss, interim director of galleries and exhibitions; John Axtell, director of marketing and public relations; Heather Cleary and Derek McMullen, Millard Sheets Library; and Kate McNamara, director of galleries and exhibitions, who inherited this project and gracefully saw it through to the end. And last but not least, I want to extend embracing arms of gratitude to my fellow instructor Joan Takayama-Ogawa and the many students from the Clay in LA class (Creative Action course), who transcribed filmed interviews and assembled the components of a three-minute film on the life of Ralph Bacerra; the names of all participating students can be found on page 134.

Crucial to the realization of this project was the generosity of the private and institutional lenders who shared their artworks with the public for the duration of the exhibition. Their names are listed on page 133. We are grateful to the directors, curators, and collection managers at the lending institutions for their efficient and collegial execution of the loan requests. In addition, several lenders or their representatives arranged to assist Otis with packing and shipping as a cost-saving measure, and we are enormously appreciative of their support: David and Julianne Armstrong, Peter and Cindy Bass, Garth Clark and Mark Del Vecchio, Paul and Sharon Dauer, Frank Lloyd Gallery, Forrest L. Merrill and Kirk Delman, and Lin Werner.

In addition to those listed above, the following individuals offered sage advice, provided essential information, answered endless questions, and have been dedicated advocates of this project for a prolonged period, and I am very grateful for their efforts: Arleen Chikami, Garth Clark and Mark Del Vecchio, Ken Deavers, Sue Keane, John Kimmelmann, Christine Leahey, Elaine Levin, Patti Marcus, Robert Miller, Sue Nelson, Merry Norris, Don Pilcher, Leslie Rosdol, and Karen Smits. I also want to thank Karen Rapp, former director of the Vincent Price Art Museum at East Los Angeles College, for her support of the presentation of the complementary exhibition *Crossroads in Clay at Chouinard and Otis*.

The exhibition and catalog could not have been realized without the dedication and professionalism of so many individuals, and I am exceedingly grateful to each and every one who has extended a hand. The successful completion of this project has affirmed once again that we walk in the paths cleared by those who ventured before us and we stand on the shoulders of others who support us.

**JO LAURIA**
CURATOR

## LENDERS TO THE EXHIBITION

American Museum of Ceramic Art
  (AMOCA)
Arizona State University Art
  Museum
David and Julianne Armstrong
George and Connie Bacerra
Peter and Cindy Bass / Cindy Lee
  Bass, Executor of the Ralph
  Bacerra Estate
Lois and Robert Boardman
Wendy Barrie Brotman and
  David Brotman
Garth Clark and Mark Del Vecchio
Mary Coquillard
Paul and Sharon Dauer
Ken Deavers
Lucille H. Epstein
Bronya and Andy Galef
Sonny and Gloria Kamm
Sue Wilson Keane
Saul E. Levi

Long Beach Museum of Art
Alan Mandell
Patti and Mike Marcus
Forrest L. Merrill
Douglas Moreland
Ted Rowland
Anne Cohen Ruderman and
  David Ruderman
Porntip Sangvanich
Ava Shire
Karen Smits
Susan Steinhauser and
  Daniel Greenberg
Dr. and Mrs. Terasaki
Lin Werner

Several private collectors who wish
to remain anonymous

## DONORS TO THE EXHIBITION AND CATALOG

### PLATINUM DONORS

Lois Boardman and The Boardman
  Family Foundation
Friends of Contemporary Ceramics
Lillian P. Lovelace
National Endowment for the Arts
Otis Board of Governors
Pasadena Art Alliance
Karen Smits
Joan Takayama-Ogawa and
  Steven K. Ogawa
Typecraft, Inc., Pasadena, California

### GOLD DONORS

Japan Art Foundation, Los Angeles
Sue Wilson Keane
Trish McGuigan
Donald W. Pilcher
Porntip Sangvanich
Anna Silver
Jeffrey Spahn
Lin Werner

### SILVER DONORS

Barbara B. Campbell
Arleen Chikami
Laura G. Cutler
Cassandra Elliot
Jo Lauria and Michael Fargo
Sidney B. Felsen and
  Joni Moisant Weyl
Keiko Fukazawa
Phyllis Green
Andre Khachtourians
Karen E. Koblitz
Christine Leahey
Elaine G. Levin
Marilyn Levin
Brent Maire
Raulee Marcus
Donald M. Pattison
Stephen Rivers
Leslie A. Rosdol
Sybil W. Stoller
Sorrarin Tantiwatyanont
  and Vivat Phanyatrakul

Opposite: **Ralph Bacerra**, *Untitled Bowl*, n.d. Ceramic.
Height: 3 in. (7.6 cm); diameter: 5 in. (12.7 cm).

Right: **Ralph Bacerra**, *Untitled Bowl*, n.d. Ceramic. Height: 3
in. (7.6 cm); diameter: 5 in. (12.7 cm).

## Student Participants in the Ralph Bacerra Project

### CREATIVE ACTION
### CLAY IN LA, FALL 2013

Alysha Aguilar

Mynor Chinchilla

Hye Min Choi

Jessica Flor

Arpine Keurjikian

Nicole Kim

Yijia Liu

Pedro Obando

Eun Jung Park

Kenza Schnur

Min Shin

Erin Watson

Yanhan Zeng

### CREATIVE ACTION
### CLAY IN LA, SPRING 2014

Osvaldo Alvarez

Judith Amaya

Curtis Back

Carli Bjerke

David Brick

Lynn Choi

Sadaf Foroutani Yazdi

Ashley Galindo

Heuiwoo Lee

Tiffany Li

Xiaoke Lu

Emilio Luarca

Cameron Mott

Ellen Park

Vassilios Pavlou

Wendi Song

Gregory Toothacre

Po-Chiang Tseng

Misa Yamada

Wenxi Zhu

### CREATIVE ACTION
### CLAY IN LA, FALL 2014

Esther Choi

Jisu Choi

Un Young Chong

Amy Faigin

Jamie Guan

Alix Gutierrez

Charles Kendall

Jina Kwon

Bo La Lee

Wenshi Lu

Mina Martinez

Jacob Moranville

Yumi Park

YunHee Park

Anjali Read

Geavanna Torres

### CREATIVE ACTION,
### CLAY IN LA, SPRING 2015

Lin Chang

Michael Chen

In-Hee Chung

Bryan Feld

Sheylee Jessica Garcia Hsu

Mason Heinold

Yoon Sang Kim

Anthony Le

Kelly Lim

King Omar Nigoza

Sujeong Park

Joseph Rubin

Adam Shinn

Stacey Song

Jasmine Ung

Yuanyuan Zhu

# Contributors

## JEANNINE FALINO

Jeannine Falino is an author, lecturer, and independent curator based in New York. Her recent exhibitions include *What Would Mrs. Webb Do? A Founder's Vision* (Museum of Arts and Design, New York, 2014), *Crafting Modernism: Midcentury American Art and Design* (Museum of Arts and Design, 2011), and *Edge of the Sublime: Enamels by Jamie Bennett* (Fuller Craft Museum, Brockton, MA, 2008). She was cocurator of *Gilded New York: Design, Fashion, and Society* (Museum of the City of New York, 2013) and *Artistic Luxury: Fabergé, Tiffany, Lalique* (Cleveland Museum of Art, 2008). Falino teaches the history of American ceramics at the Rhode Island School of Design.

## HOLLIS GOODALL

Hollis Goodall is curator of Japanese art at the Los Angeles County Museum of Art. She has worked at the museum since 1981 and has overseen some 270 installations of the permanent collection and special exhibitions, including those treating ceramics, lacquer, painting, prints, book art, kimono, netsuke, and photography. She is the author of numerous publications, including, most recently, *Living for the Moment: Japanese Prints from the Barbara S. Bowman Collection* (Los Angeles County Museum of Art, 2015). Goodall received a BA (with honors) from the University of Texas in 1977 and an MA in East Asian art from the University of Kansas, followed by two years as a research fellow at the University of Kyoto in Japan.

## CHRISTY JOHNSON

Christy Johnson is director emerita of the American Museum of Ceramic Art (AMOCA), Pomona, CA. She holds a BA in English literature from California State University, Los Angeles, and later studied studio art at Otis Art Institute under Ralph Bacerra and at Pasadena City College with Phil Cornelius. At AMOCA, she curated exhibitions on American art tile, California-made dinnerware, *tenmoku* glazes, and well-known ceramic artists such as Rudy Autio, Don Reitz, Paul Soldner, Peter Voulkos, and Patti Warashina. Johnson participated in the Getty's Pacific Standard Time initiative, producing a critically acclaimed exhibition and book titled *Common Ground: Ceramics in Southern California 1945–1975* (AMOCA, 2011).

## JO LAURIA

Jo Lauria is a Los Angeles–based curator and writer who received her curatorial training in decorative arts at the Los Angeles County Museum of Art. She is a design and crafts specialist and author of several historical survey books and many essays and articles. Most recently, Lauria organized the exhibitions *Honoring the Past, Embracing the Future* (American Museum of Ceramic Art, Pomona, CA, 2015) and *Peter Shire: Public Work, Lines of Desire* (Architecture and Design Museum, Los Angeles, 2014). Lauria received a BA from Yale University, an MA from Loyola Marymount, and an MFA from Otis College of Art and Design, where she studied ceramics with Ralph Bacerra.

**Ralph Bacerra**, *Untitled Stacking Box*, c. late 1980s. Porcelain, overglaze enamel, and metallic luster. Height: 12 in. (30.5 cm); diameter: 5 in. (12.7 cm). Collection of Lin Werner.

Overleaf: **Ralph Bacerra**, *Untitled Plate*, 2005. Ceramic. Height: 2 in. (5.1 cm); diameter: 22½ in. (57.2 cm). Collection of Wendy Barrie Brotman and David Brotman.